MANUAL COMMUNICATION

FINGERSPELLING AND THE LANGUAGE OF SIGNS

BARBARA E. BABBINI

A Course of Study Outline for Students

UNIVERSITY OF ILLINOIS PRESS

Urbana Chicago London

PREFACE

The present course of study outline was prepared for use by students in classes taught by instructors using the book, Manual Communication, a Course of Study Outline for Instructors, by Babbini (1973). The material herein is coordinated with that in the instructor's manual and is designed for use primarily as a workbook for out-of-class review and practice on material which has already been covered in class. It is not intended to be a book from which a student can learn new signs he has not yet been taught or seen demonstrated in class, and students are cautioned not to attempt to use it for this purpose.

The word-descriptions of signs contained in this workbook are intended to assist the student in recalling specific signs they have already been taught in class, or have seen their instructor demonstrate, in the event such signs are forgotten or cannot be recalled with precision. The practice material is designed to reinforce what the student has learned in class by affording practice in using letters, numbers, and signs in words or sentences as they would normally be used in conversing with deaf people in the language of signs and fingerspelling.

Also included in the present manual are homework assignments which involve: (1) student composition of sentences using words for which signs have been taught, which students should practice and bring to class for recital purposes; (2) student composition of sentences using words which will be taught in the next lesson, and including words for which signs have already been taught, for the purpose of encouraging active participation by students in the classroom learning processes as well as practice; and (3) outside assignments which, if the instructor assigns them, require the student to make himself familiar with the activities of the deaf people in the local communities, become acquainted with at least one deaf adult in said communities, and, through his study of the activities and people in the local deaf communities, plan some kind of a hypothetical service project which would in some way be of benefit to the deaf people in the community whether by providing a service not currently provided, by improving an existing service, or by making it possible for deaf people to expand their social, educational, or cultural contacts with hearing people--including the students in manual communication classes, who, in any event, need the practice in manual communication such contacts with deaf people would provide.

The student will find in the present manual other helpful information which will provide him with certain fundamental knowledge about the language of signs and fingerspelling, its history, its idiosyncratic variations, and some of the subcultural aspects of what is commonly called the "deaf world." Also included is a lengthy bibliography of books, articles, and films on the language of signs and fingerspelling, some of which the student may wish to obtain for reference or practice purposes, or simply to increase his knowledgeability about deaf people and their world.

iii

iv

Since the present manual was an outgrowth of the companion manual, <u>Manual Communication, a Course of Study Outline for Instructors</u> (Babbini, 1973), it stands to reason that without the help of the people who gave of their time, energy, expertise, and encouragement in the development of the instructor's manual, the present manual might never have been born. To these same people, again, the author's gratitude is due, and hereby tendered. Special thanks are due the following:

Dr. Ray L. Jones, Director, Leadership Training Program in the Area of the Deaf, San Fernando Valley State College, Northridge, California; Miss Virginia Vail, Principal (ret.), University High School, Westwood, California; Dr. Stephen P. Quigley, Professor, Acting Director of IREC, University of Illinois, Urbana, Illinois; Mr. Kenneth E. Brasel, Doctoral Student, University of Illinois, and Instructor, Manual Communication Classes, Illinois State University, Normal, Illinois; Mr. Jon Rawleigh, formerly of the TV staff at the National Technical Institute for the Deaf, Rochester, New York; Mr. Zoltan Ujhelyi, Television Engineer, University of Illinois, Urbana, Illinois; Mrs. Irene Lamkin, Miss Marilyn Brasel, and Miss Carla Donaldson, Secretaries, IREC, University of Illinois, Urbana, Illinois.

And to all the students who have passed through the author's classes over the years.

Barbara E. Babbini

CONTENTS

vi

viii

A BRIEF HISTORY OF THE LANGUAGE OF SIGNS

The antecedents of the modern language of signs are buried in the mists of antiquity, but one thing is clear: from earliest recorded history, it is known that gestures (or signs) have been employed for communication between groups of people of dissimilar languages and cultures throughout the ages up to and including the present. Gesture language, therefore, is one of the oldest--if not the oldest--means of communication between human beings.

It stands to reason that some form of rudimentary gesture language must surely have been used by people in antiquity in communicating with deaf people, but the idea that a gesture language could be developed to the point where it could be used as a formal method of communicating does not seem to have occurred to anyone until the sixteenth century. Part of the reason for this appears to be the generally accepted theory that deaf people were uneducable. They were thought to be incapable of reasoning, of having ideas or opinions, and, in some cultures, they were considered to be possessed of the devil, or in the bad graces of the gods. They were, therefore, figures of fun, scorned, reviled--or even feared. It would have been a brave person indeed who would consider going against the prevailing public opinion and putting the theory to the test.

In the sixteenth century, however, a brave person emerged in the person of Girolamo Cardano, an Italian physician, who raised his voice to dispute the theory that deaf people were uneducable. Cardano held that the hearing of words was not necessary for the understanding of ideas, and devised a code for teaching deaf people which, unfortunately, was never put into use. However, his words fell on fertile ground, and, although slow to germinate, eventually began sprouting, and paving the way for dispelling the attitude that deaf people were incapable of learning.

It was in Spain that the first successful attempts to educate deaf individuals were made. A Spanish monk, Pedro Ponce de Leon, succeeded in educating the deaf children of several noble Spanish families so that they could be declared legally qualified to inherit the estates of their families. Spanish law at that time was such that a person, in order to inherit property, had to be literate--to be able to read and write--and de Leon succeeded in providing his deaf pupils with these skills. The theory that deaf people were uneducable, therefore, was disproved.

It is interesting to note, also, that de Leon apparently was able to teach his pupils to speak in addition to teaching them to read and write. Presumably he was also able to teach them to read lips in the process of teaching them to speak, but these skills apparently were interesting ancilliary benefits obtained by the deaf children after the good monk had accomplished the main task required of him by his noble employers--that of teaching their deaf heirs to read and write so that they could inherit the family estates.

1

Some time later, Juan Martin Pablo Bonet developed the one-handed manual alphabet, which has descended almost unchanged to that used today. Bonet also wrote a book on education of deaf people, in which both the manual alphabet and some signs were advocated as the method whereby the tutor could communicate with his pupils while providing them with an education.

While individuals like de Leon and Bonet were pioneers in the sense that they proved that deaf persons could be educated, and that a formal gesture language could be employed for the purpose of communicating with deaf people in the process of educating them, their success was limited to a few select individuals to whom they acted as tutors. Education of deaf people, therefore, was restricted to the very rich, or those of royal blood, for only they could afford private tutors for their deaf children. It was in France and Germany that public education of deaf children began. It was also in those two countries that the methods controversy was born—the argument over whether deaf children should be taught with or without the employment of the language of signs—an argument which has persisted to this day.

In France, Abbe Charles de l'Epee founded the first public school for deaf children. In addition to being considered the father of public education for deaf children, Abbe de l'Epee is also regarded as the father of the modern language of signs. Abee de l'Epee was convinced that sign language was the "natural language" of deaf people, and held that their education should be based on the use of this "natural" language. However, the language of signs as used by deaf people of that day was rudimentary, and the Abbe recognized that the crude signs employed by deaf people of the time were too limited for use as tools in an educational program. He, therefore, attempted to develop and refine the existing language of signs into a full language which could be more effectively used in educating deaf people. The language of signs used today has been derived in a large part from that developed by Abbe de l'Epee, although it has undergone considerable refinement in the years since the good Abbe first put it into use.

Samuel Heinicke was Germany's counterpart of France's Abbe de l'Epee. Heinicke, however, shared only two of the Abbe's convictions—his belief that deaf people were educable and that they could be educated in public education programs. In contrast to de l'Epee, however, Heinicke believed that deaf people could be educated through speechreading alone. He, therefore, was the forerunner of modern-day advocates of the so-called oral method of instruction (called the German method in Heinicke's day and for some time afterward). Heinicke's philosophy still forms the basic foundation for the belief in the oral method, although his methods of teaching have also undergone many changes and refinements over the years.

Education of deaf children in the United States can be considered to have begun with the arrival upon the scene of Thomas Hopkins Gallaudet. A minister, Gallaudet was approached by Dr. Mason Cogswell, whose daughter, Alice, was deaf. Dr. Cogswell had heard that deaf children were successfully being educated in Europe, and wished Gallaudet to journey to England to learn the methods being employed there to teach deaf children such as his little girl. From this request was born the career of a man who was to become one of the most famous educators of the deaf in the world, a man who was also responsible for the introduction of the language of signs into the United States.

Gallaudet's plan on departing for England was to study the English methods of instructing deaf children, then to extend his trip into France where he would study the French methods. He planned then to select the best of both methods, and combine them in a comprehensive plan for educating deaf children in America, beginning with little Alice Cogswell.

Unfortunately, when he outlined his plans to the English educators of the deaf, they reacted by refusing him permission to learn their methods unless he agreed to abandon his plan to study the French methods and combine only the best of the two. (It is ironic that this reaction is still common today in the late twentieth century, for there are pockets of blind belief in one method of instruction over all others, and proponents of such methods are apt to be adamant in insisting that their method be used in its entirety, with no contamination from other methods permitted—and prospective students who wish to study the method, but will not promise to adhere strictly to that method to the exclusion of all others, often find it difficult to obtain permission to enroll.)

After several months of frustrating negotiations with the English experts, an event occurred which caused Gallaudet to give up his plans to study in England. Abbe Sicard, a noted educator of deaf people in France, arrived in England on a lecture tour with two of his most outstanding pupils, one of whom was a young man by the name of Laurent Clerc. Gallaudet attended one of the lectures given by Sicard, and was so impressed by the ability of the two deaf pupils, Clerc in particular, that he immediately abandoned his negotiations with the English and went to Paris to study with Sicard.

At the conclusion of his studies, Gallaudet returned to America, bringing with him Laurent Clerc. Clerc subsequently became the first deaf teacher of the deaf in America, and he helped Gallaudet found the first school for the deaf in this country, the American Asylum for the Deaf and Dumb in Hartford, Connecticut, which subsequently became the American School for the Deaf.

Since the French method of instruction involved the use of the language of signs, Gallaudet brought back with him a knowledge of this form of communication, a skill he and Laurent Clerc taught to others. From this beginning, the language of signs spread rapidly to all corners of the country, and soon was known by nearly every deaf person from one end of the country to the other.

In time, other methods of instructing deaf children came into the country—those which did not employ the language of signs, and, in fact, forbade its use—but the language of signs was firmly established among deaf people themselves by then, and has remained the national language of deaf people in America. Despite over a hundred years of repeated efforts to eradicate it or to stop its steady spread to each new generation of deaf people—even to those who are supposedly isolated from such "contamination" by rigid rules designed to prevent its being learned by deaf children—only a few deaf adults today fail to acquire the ability to use sign language somewhere along the way, and to make it part and parcel of their communicative lives.

4

Gallaudet, in bringing the language of signs to our country, released the lid of a Pandora's box of troubles for later oral method advocates, a lid nobody has ever since been able to force shut again. But for deaf people, his release of the lid opened up a means of communication with the world around them, and they, themselves, have since developed and refined it until it is today a classical, beautiful, and picturesque language of gesture in which the great majority of deaf people communicate their thoughts and feelings to each other--and to those hearing people who have taken the trouble to learn the language of signs.

The language of signs is idiomatic; it incorporates pantomime; it is individualistic--and sometimes highly confusing to a beginner. But it is always interesting; and a student in the language of signs will find it greatly rewarding as he progresses to better and better communication with his deaf pupils, co-workers, clients, relatives, and friends. Such a student may, if he persists in learning the language of signs with all its subtleties, nuances, and idiosyncracies, eventually become so fluent that he can help his deaf compatriots in one of the most vital ways a hearing person can help deaf people-- by interpreting for deaf people, and opening the door for deaf people to experience at first hand the audible events which go in the sometimes baffling world of the hearing.

Bibliography source: Quigley, S. P. Historical background, education of the deaf. In Education of the Deaf. A report to the President by the Advisory Committee on Education of the Deaf in the United States. U.S. Government Printing Office, 1965.

INTRODUCTION

I. Why Learn Manual Communication?

The student who enrolls in a beginning course in manual communication may have any one of a wide variety of reasons for deciding he wants or needs to learn how to communicate with deaf people by manual means. He may be an aspirant to an occupation in which he will work with deaf people; he may have deaf relatives or co-workers; he may be the parent of a deaf child; he may be a professional worker whose job brings him into frequent contact with deaf people; he may have friends who are deaf; he may be a minister who discovers deaf people among his parishoners; he may have watched a television show, or a movie, or read a book about deaf people; or he may simply have wandered in off the street, so to speak, intrigued by the novelty of learning a new form of communication between human beings. A student may have only one reason, or any number of reasons, for wanting to learn manual communication, but whatever his reason, or reasons, the underlying motivation behind any student's enrolling in a class in manual communication is primarily a desire to learn how to talk with deaf people on his hands, to bridge the communication barrier between his own world of sound and the silent or muffled world of deaf people.

Deaf people are very dependent upon people who can hear and who can also use manual methods of communicating. Without these people, those who cannot hear, or hear imperfectly, regardless of their oral communication skills in speech or speechreading, would remain in a glass cage of isolation, seeing and being seen, but excluded from and not understanding much if not most of the countless human interactions which take place every minute of every day in every society in the world. Whereas other handicaps cut people off from things, from doing things, or from having things, deafness cuts a person off from people. It cuts one off from communicating with one's fellow man, from exchanging with other people one's ideas, feelings, moods, thoughts, and information, and excludes one from all or most of the other language-based dynamics of human relationships which are dependent upon one's ability to communicate easily and effectively with one's fellow man--unless a visual means of communication is provided and employed.

For the great majority of people who suffered hearing impairment early in life, before language and communication skills were developed, oral communication skills seldom develop to the point where they can be used to bridge the communication gap between the deaf person and all other people in his environment. At best, communication is limited, labored, and all too frequently distorted in both expression and reception, and all but impossible with strangers who are not familiar with the deaf person. Consequently, prelingually deafened people remain largely isolated, cut off from the socializing influences exerted by the hundreds of thousands of auditory stimuli impinging every moment upon the ears and brains of those not similarly handicapped--unless those stimuli can be transformed somehow into meaningful and accurate visual stimuli.

6

The deaf person must make his eyes accomplish what his ears cannot--acquaint him with the world about him, its norms, mores, its people, and their language. If the information his eyes give him about the world is inadequate, distorted, or puzzling, and if he is, in addition, hampered by inadequate speech skills, he is blocked from testing his conclusions about events in his world through the medium of putting his conclusions into words and then comparing them with the reactions and conclusions of others regarding the same events. His perceptions of the world, therefore, tend to become, and remain, distorted and defective; his written and spoken language will often be bizarre in structure as well as in enunciation; his reactions and responses to situations will frequently be regarded as immature or puzzlingly atypical; and he will often be considered to be mentally as well as socially retarded even though he usually is found to possess normal intelligence when tested on nonverbal IQ tests. On the other hand, when he is given a means of communicating easily, meaningfully, and effectively with those in his world whose perceptions are unhindered by an auditory handicap and thus likely to be more accurate, he becomes able to exercise his innate intelligence to test and retest his perceptions, to gradually modify them to closer approximations of reality than is possible when communication is restricted and difficult, and he then becomes able to conform easily and acceptably to expected standards of human social behavior.

The foregoing should not be taken to mean that all deaf people are immature, unsophisticated, socially inadequate, and/or deficient in language and communication skills. Far from it. Despite their handicap, most deaf people do acquire a measure of maturity in the sense that they conform to most norms of social behavior, and they do develop the ability to use language even if the form of language used may still be somewhat deviant in grammatical syntax and structure. They may even develop fairly good oral communication skills which they can use in communicating with nondeaf people who do not know how to use the language of signs and fingerspelling. However, with few exceptions, even those deaf people who have excellent oral skills, good language abilities, and considerable social sophistication find it far easier to interact with those who know and can communicate by manual methods than with those who cannot. Few deaf adults fail to learn manual communication at some time or another in their lives, and almost all of those who learn the method use it by preference among themselves and with those hearing people who have also learned this form of communication. It is far more expressive, and accurate, as a communication medium than are speech and speechreading--and far less taxing to the receptive visual skills of the deaf person regardless of how well the deaf person may be able to read lips.

Manual communication, therefore, is a skill well worth acquiring if a person wishes to communicate with deaf people by the most effective and meaningful method extant, whatever the person's reasons for wishing to learn such communication may be. It is not hard to learn, but neither is it easy. It requires developing muscles in one's fingers and arms that one was not aware one possessed; it requires considerable mental gymnastics to learn to sort out rapidly changing handshapes and perceive a word where there were formerly only a jumble of isolated letters; a sentence where there were a meaningless collection of movements of hands and arms; a concept disguised in a particular pattern of signs; a mood where there was only a lifted eyebrow or a slight exaggeration of movement as a clue. It requires analyses of the grammatical structure of language patterns used by deaf people, for they are reflected in the grammatical patterns of the language of signs; it requires a tremendous amount of memorization--and practice, practice, practice. One cannot become adept in using it in the space of a few weeks. or months. It usually takes years to become fluent in it, years of frequent association and practice with deaf people themselves. However, the basic skills can be learned in a semester or two, skills which will provide the student with a readily utilizable means of communicating with deaf people which, despite initial limitations, will be far more effective than oral communication alone. The basic skills will also provide the foundation upon which the student himself can build his understanding of deaf people as well as his proficiency in "their" language, the language of signs.

II.   So _You_ Want to Learn Manual Communication.

You Have to Practice!

So _you_ want to learn manual communication? Congratulations! You are about to embark on a task, the result of which will offer many rewards in the form of increased effectiveness in communicating with your deaf friends, co-workers, clients, pupils, children, parishioners, relatives--and with strangers who happen to be deaf; rewards in the form of gratitude from deaf people whose lives you will enrich by opening the doors of communication for them so that they may see into your world; rewards in new friendships you will acquire as a result of becoming a member of the select group of people who can use manual communication; and, finally, a sometimes debatable reward in the form of the "Open Sesame" you will be granted almost automatically into a society composed of what one expert has called, "The most misunderstood of men, but the gamest of them all"--the deaf people of today's world, and those who live and work with them.

It is assumed that, since you are reading this book, you have enrolled in a class in manual communication. This is the best way to start learning manual communication--if you did not happen to be born to deaf parents (in which case you would hardly be reading a manual for beginning and intermediate students). However, there are certain responsibilities involved in a student's mastering the fundamentals of manual communication, some of which are the responsibilities of the instructor, but others of which rest squarely on the student's shoulders, or, in other words, on _you_.

The instructor has the responsibility of seeing that you learn expressive and receptive fingerspelling and signing, or, to put it in other words, he has the responsibility of seeing that you can both correctly execute all fingerspelled letters and all signs he teaches you (_expressive_ skills) and can recognize them when someone else uses them whether individually or in sentences (_receptive_ skills). However, he cannot in the space of a few hours of classroom work each week, make sure that you _retain_ the signs he has taught you, for retention of learned material, particularly signs, entails far more repetition and reinforcement than the instructor will have time to provide you with as an individual student in a class of anywhere from ten to thirty other

students, all of whom will need their share of the instructor's time and
attention, too. This means that the instructor cannot do all the work; you
have to do most of the work yourself in developing your expressive skills,
while the instructor concentrates his skills on the task he is best suited
to help you with--development of your receptive ability in manual communication.

What the instructor will do is devote most of the classroom time to the
rapid development of your ability to understand what is said in the language
of signs and fingerspelling, for this will be the most difficult part of
your learning task. He can do this because he can administer receptive
drills and tests to the whole class at the same time, whereas he can only
help one student at a time with the student's expressive skills. To be
sure, you will receive help and training in developing your expressive skills
and help in overcoming any errors in technique or faulty habits you may develop, but there will simply not be enough time for you, as an individual
student, to be given the amount of individual attention and practice you will
need. A tremendous number of repetitions will be required before a given
sign will become a permanent part of your expressive vocabulary of signs and
can be retrieved automatically when you need it--and there are over 600 signs
in this course alone, which you will have to learn and practice repeatedly
until you "automatize" them in your repertoire.

By the same token, the instructor cannot practice your fingerspelling for
you. He can see that you shape the letters correctly; help you overcome or
avoid common technical flaws of delivery; drill you along with your fellow
students in the clear and errorless fingerspelling of words; teach you short-
cuts which will speed up your fingerspelling; and train you in vocalizing
the words simultaneously with your fingerspelling of the same words--but his
primary task is to drill intensively the whole class as a group in receptive
fingerspelling. He will not be able to help you build up speed unless you
practice, practice, and then practice some more. When you practice, you
gradually build up the ability to automatically retrieve (and produce) the
handshape of any letter of the alphabet without undue stumbling or hesitat-
ing or searching of your memory. And, as you "automate" this process, speed
in fingerspelling builds up naturally. If all of the students in a class
practice enough, the instructor's job is made much easier, and more efficient
in that he can employ a wider variety of fingerspelling drills, games, and
other techniques whereby the students themselves help train each other in
receptive fingerspelling. A few students who do not practice can hold back
the whole class, for their slow fingerspelling offers little challenge and
practically no training in reception to their fellow students--yet, in all
fairness, they must still be afforded the opportunity for in-class practice
during games and drills, for it is primarily at this time that the instructor
must assess their individual progress.

The reason why the importance of out-of-class practice in fingerspelling
is stressed is that learning to read fingerspelling on the hands of another
person is, without question, the most difficult task facing the student in
a manual communication class. Learning expressive fingerspelling, ironically,
is probably the easiest to learn, but it is also most neglected by students
practicing at home, for signs are usually more captivating, interesting, and

Then, when you learn the signs in Lesson 3, you can add even more complexity to the sentences you compose:

6. <u>Please</u> <u>excuse</u> <u>me</u>, <u>I</u> <u>didn't</u> <u>understand</u> <u>what</u> <u>you</u> <u>said</u>.

7. <u>Say</u> <u>that</u> again, <u>please</u>, <u>I'm</u> <u>sorry</u> <u>but</u> <u>I</u> <u>didn't</u> <u>understand</u>.

After Lesson 4, in addition to learning how to sign some words which you previously had to fingerspell, you can add practice sentences which include the new signs:

8. <u>I</u> <u>must</u> <u>practice</u> <u>more</u>, for <u>I</u> am so <u>slow</u>.

9. <u>Will</u> <u>you</u> <u>please</u> <u>say</u> <u>that</u> <u>again</u>? <u>I</u> <u>think</u> <u>I</u> got <u>confused</u>.

10. <u>I'm</u> <u>sorry</u> <u>I</u> am <u>slow</u> (or <u>dumb</u>, or <u>confused</u>), <u>but</u> <u>would</u> <u>you</u> <u>say</u> <u>that</u> <u>again</u>, <u>slowly</u>, <u>please</u>?

11. Where <u>did</u> <u>you</u> go <u>to</u> <u>school</u>?

12. Do <u>you</u> <u>have</u> any children?

13. Do <u>you</u> <u>work</u>? <u>What</u> is <u>your</u> <u>job</u>?

14. <u>Slow</u> down, <u>please</u>, <u>I'm</u> getting <u>confused</u> <u>again</u>.

15. <u>I</u> <u>understood</u> <u>your</u> <u>signs</u>, <u>but</u> <u>I</u> <u>didn't</u> <u>understand</u> <u>your</u> <u>finger-spelling</u>.

16. <u>Thank</u> <u>you</u> <u>for</u> <u>talking</u> <u>to</u> <u>me</u>.

Another good way to insure yourself of sufficient practice in all of the signs you have been taught is to use the Master Vocabulary List in the Appendix as a tally sheet. Each time you compose a sentence using a given sign, make a small tally-mark alongside that sign--and you will soon be able to discern at a glance which signs you have been practicing regularly-- and which ones you need to practice more by composing sentences which include the neglected sign.

There is no hard-and-fast rule governing the number of times you must use a given sign before you can safely be said to have "automatized" it to the point where you can recall and use it without having to stop and think about how it is made. A good rule of thumb to follow is: If you have to hesitate, even momentarily, before making the sign when using it in a sentence, you have not practiced <u>using</u> the sign often enough. The same applies if you find yourself frequently having to fingerspell the word for the sign instead of signing it, or using another sign in its place by mistake.

Most students can readily recall <u>individual</u> signs when presented with the single word for the sign, but it is only those who have practiced using the signs <u>in sentences</u> a sufficient number of times who find the signs coming automatically to their minds (and hands) when such signs are embedded in sentences along with other signs and fingerspelled words. Until you can accomplish this, your delivery in manual communication will remain halting, jerky, and nonfluent regardless of how beautifully you can execute the individual signs and fingerspelled words. In addition, you will find it difficult to concentrate on another vital aspect of your learning--that of adding <u>expressiveness</u>, <u>mood</u>, and <u>inflection</u> to your signing--when your attention is occupied primarily with trying to recall how signs are made against the competition and distraction posed by the need to use the appropriate facial expression, pausing, and emphasis required by the context and mood of the sentence you are trying to convey.

Adding Expressiveness to Your Ability to Use Manual Communication

When you are talking with <u>any</u> deaf person, you will be struck by one characteristic all deaf persons display in common--they all keep their eyes on you. This is not simply because he <u>has</u> to in order to see what you are saying on your hands (although he does have to keep his eyes on you). If you will study his eyes closely, however, you will see that they are not simply following your signing and fingerspelling, but are focused primarily upon your <u>face</u>, <u>eyes</u>, and <u>lips</u>. In fact, he will do this even if he is not paying particular attention to what you are saying--or even if he cannot understand you very well.

What the deaf person is doing with his eyes is searching for clues <u>in addition</u> to the actual words in your message. He looks at your lips for your specific meaning for the sign you are using, for lipreading reinforcement of the word you are fingerspelling, and for smiles, tightness, lip-licking, lip-biting--all of which are some of the clues to your <u>mood</u> that he is seeking, and he looks at your eyes for the same thing. The shifting eyes of nervousness, the smiling eyes of pleasure, the staring eyes of fright, the glassy-eyes of boredom, the impish eyes of mischief and teasing, the overly innocent eyes of a deliberate fraud: all help him to decide what interpretation he should put on your message <u>regardless</u> of the actual wording you use. He looks for nods or shakes of the head, shrugs of the shoulder, indecisive hesitation, emphatic force, small frowns or smiles (or big ones), seriousness or lack of it, or, in general, a whole matrix of nonverbal clues most people are not aware they are giving when they talk. If the deaf person could <u>hear</u> you talk, he would pick up some of these nonverbal cues from the tone and inflection in your speech. But, since he cannot hear, he must pick them up visually--even as he sends his own cues to you by <u>visible</u> facial and body expressions and movements.

The task here is to learn <u>to use those clues deliberately</u> to help him understand exactly what you mean, what your mood is, thus enabling him to respond appropriately. Where a person with normal hearing will find many clues to the emotions of a speaker from the tone and inflection of his voice while he is speaking, even if the speaker betrays nothing of this in his face, eyes, body posture or movements, a deaf person cannot obtain his cues in this way. He has to use his eyes--and he can often pick up tiny clues that a person with normal hearing would miss. However, even if he were so skilled at this that he could detect the mood of a dead-pan signer in spite of the signer's expressionless face (which not all deaf persons are able to do), he does not enjoy talking with such a signer any more than a hearing person enjoys talking with someone who speaks in a flat, expressionless voice regardless of the emotional context of whatever it is he is saying. Facial expression, force, speed, and bodily gestures, therefore, are to manual communication what tone, inflection, volume, and timbre are to speech. They give _life_ and _meaning_ to the communication taking place.

Communication also happens to be a two-way street. It is not sufficient that a student in manual communication develop the ability to express himself both technically and emotionally in signs and fingerspelling. He must also learn to read clues on the _deaf person's_ face, and this is sometimes harder to learn to do than to learn to put expressiveness in one's own signing. Because deaf persons have usually had years of frustration behind them, frustration they have had to swallow and hide behind agreeable smiles and nods, they are usually rather accomplished at hiding their feelings, and even at pretending they understand when actually they do not. The student, therefore, may blithely assume he is being fully accepted and understood because the deaf person is smiling and nodding his head, when in truth he has reserved judgment about the student and has not understood a darn thing he said. Unfortunately, this is as true of children as of adult deaf persons, for the frustration cycle begins before the child even enters school. By the time he has entered school, he is usually adept at disguising feelings which he has gotten into trouble for showing in earlier years, and is an accomplished little faker when it comes to pretending comprehension when he has none.

Not all of the appearance of understanding is, indeed, pretense. Quite often the deaf person is merely waiting, searching for the key word, the key clue which will make a largely incomprehensible statement suddenly clear. And often the deaf person has misunderstood--but _thinks_ he understands. The student, therefore, must search for clues on the deaf person's _face_, in the _way_ he gives his responses, as well as in the actual words in which he couches his responses. The student who does not attend to these clues is going to find himself constantly making assumptions about a conversation with a deaf person, and about the deaf person himself, which all too often will bear little relationship to reality.

The rule to be garnered from the above is: _Make every effort to help the deaf person obtain visual clues as to your mood and meaning--and keep your own eyes on the deaf person so that you will pick up similar clues from him._ Your instructor will help you with the former, but only practice with _real live deaf persons_ will develop your ability to correctly interpret the latter. Manual communication is _communication_, and it cannot be fully learned in the classroom any more than surgery can be learned from books, lectures, and demonstrations. Just as a doctor must practice and polish his skills by carving up an actual human body, a manual communications student must eventually practice and polish his skills by conversing with deaf people.

One thing you can do to help yourself acquire expressiveness in your signing and fingerspelling, however, is to practice in front of a mirror at home. You should compose a series of emotionally loaded sentences, then practice them in front of a mirror. At first, you will be concentrating so hard on how to make each sign and fingerspell each word that you will not be able to evaluate your own performance from the standpoint of appropriateness of the facial expression and emotion you are displaying while delivering the sentence. But, once the signs and fingerspelling of the sentence have been mastered, you should attend to your face and see if you are conveying the appropriate mood. If it does not seem quite right, you can then practice in a slightly different fashion. Say the sentence aloud, packing as much emotion as possible into it, and watch what your face does while you do this. Then say the sentence without using your voice and try to evaluate whether another person would be able to evaluate your mood if all he could see was what you see in the mirror--your face and silently moving lips. Still another way of practicing expressiveness is to think of a sentence, then pretend to be trying to convey that same sentence to another person by using nonverbal communication alone--no lip movements, no voice, no signs; nothing but your eyes, face, and body. If you are skilled in drama--particularly method acting--this should be an easy task. If not, then you will have to develop the talent if you ever wish to become truly fluent in manual communication.

III. Do's and Don'ts, and "I'll Be Doggoned's"
of the Language of Signs

Do's and Don'ts:

There are certain rules that one must observe in communicating with deaf persons in the language of signs. Some of them are obvious--like making sure you are facing the deaf person, and making sure he is looking at you before you start signing, because if you do not, you are likely to end up talking to yourself, not to him. Other rules are not so obvious. To take one example: You are aware, of course, that a deaf person MUST look directly at you when you are talking with him, whatever means of communication-- oral or manual--you are using between you, but are you aware that you should look at him too? Of course, if he is using the language of signs without using his voice, you will jolly well have to look at him. BUT--and here is the sticker--some deaf people use both signs and speech at one and the same time, and it is all too easy for a person who can hear and who can understand the deaf person's speech to let his eyes wander away from the deaf person's face even if he is listening to his speech with total attention--and the deaf person thinks he has lost his audience. Common courtesy, therefore dictates that a person keep his eyes on the deaf person until he has finished what he is saying, regardless of whether he is saying it orally, manually, or in a combination of the two methods.

Another rule has to do with your attitude. This can best be stated as: Don't "talk down" to deaf people. By and large, deaf people are of normal intelligence despite any language deficiencies they may have, and the quickest way to turn them off is to attempt to patronize them. Patronization is as insulting to the deaf person as it is to a person with normal hearing, but few hearing people seem to appreciate this fact. Indignities a normally courteous hearing person would not dream of inflicting upon another hearing person, he does not hesitate to inflict upon a deaf person; and these can range from forcing unwanted help upon a deaf person who is perfectly capable of handling his own affairs, through heedless disregard for the deaf person's feeling by discussing him verbally with another hearing person as if the deaf person was not present, or were an object instead of a human being with feelings, to the insulting situation where a hearing person with whom a deaf person has been conversing allows another hearing person to interrupt the conversation without apology or explanation, and the two hearing people then proceed to exclude the deaf person by carrying on their conversation verbally.

Whether the exclusion of the deaf person is unintentional or deliberate, he can seldom follow fast verbal conversation between two hearing people by lipreading alone, so he is left standing, abandoned, with the egg of humiliation all over his face because, it seems to him, his erstwhile conversational partner apparently did not consider him interesting nor important enough to pay him the courtesy of an apology or explanation, nor intelligent enough to be included in the new conversation with the other hearing person.

If one were to imagine one's self in a similar situation in a foreign country, where one has only a limited command of the language of that country, one can begin to appreciate the resentment the deaf person feels at being abandoned and subsequently ignored while two natives--one or both of whom he knows could carry on their conversation in his language if they had chosen to do so--chatter away without a thought for his feelings.

In all honesty, it must be admitted that deaf people themselves are guilty of this breach in good manners--particularly those who have the ability to both speak and sign simultaneously--and unintentionally exclude hearing people with limited manual communication skills from their rapid manual conversations. However, the hearing person in such a situation does not normally feel insulted, and usually is quick to remind the deaf person of his limited signing skill, and asks for a vocal replay. On the other hand, the deaf person, sensitized by a lifetime of being made to feel like a second-class person, of being snubbed, ignored, and patronized both intentionally and unintentionally, does not call the social faux pas of his "betters" to their attention. Rather, he withdraws in hurt and resentment, and soon wanders away to seek more congenial--and dependable--conversational partners.

The situation just described is far from uncommon. Even veteran interpreters for deaf people sometimes forget deaf people are present, and carry on verbal conversations with other hearing people which exclude the deaf people. Generally, however, the good interpreter will soon remember, apologize, and thereafter make an attempt to keep the deaf person informed of what is being said. Sometimes the interpreter will do this by attempting to interpret what each person is saying; other times he will just sign and finger-spell his own remarks as he is making them, and trust to the deaf person's lipreading ability to pick up the other person's remarks when aided by partial knowledge of what is being discussed. If the interpreter chooses the latter approach, the good one usually will keep a weather eye on the deaf person, and if he appears to be getting lost, the interpreter brings him up to date by interpreting the remarks he did not catch.

You may be asking at this point what you, a complete newcomer to the language of signs, can do which would help you avoid a situation in which you are interrupted by another hearing person who must talk to you in front of a deaf person with whom you have been trying to communicate. It really is simple: Observe the common courtesy of apologizing for the necessary interruption. A simple "excuse me," which is one of the first signs you will learn in this course, will enable the deaf person to wait a reasonable length of time for your attention to return to him before he will start to feel abandoned for more interesting company. If you must accompany the other hearing person elsewhere, excuse yourself and give a brief explanation of why you must leave. If, on the other hand, your conversation with the other hearing person is not urgent--or private (in which case you should conduct it in another room!)--and it lasts longer than just a few minutes, you should then attempt to bring the deaf person into the conversation if he is still patiently standing around waiting for you. This is not always easy to do, particularly if the deaf person is shy, or knows his speaking ability is poor and your receptive manual communication skills limited. However, it can be done in such a way that the deaf person, whether he participates actively in the conversation or not, at least _feels_ included--and may be enabled to follow the conversation to a degree. A few fingerspelled or signed key words can narrow the conversational topic down for the deaf person to the point where his lipreading ability may enable him to catch most of what is being said.

It goes without saying that it is extremely rude for two hearing persons to carry on a verbal conversation in the presence of a deaf person IF both hearing persons are fluent in manual communication. The rudeness is intensified if, in addition, one such hearing person interrupts, without apology or explanation, a conversation between the other hearing person and the deaf person--then proceeds to engage the hearing person in a verbal conversation in which neither hearing person uses his manual communication skills, nor makes any attempt to include the deaf person regardless of how urgent the discussion between them may be.

Few deaf people forgive an insult of this sort, for they know it would take but a moment for one or the other to apologize and explain (if possible) the reason for the interruption, particularly if it results in his conversational partner leaving him to go off with the newcomer. It would be well, therefore, to keep this in mind for the time when you become fluent in manual communication, for there will be times when you will find yourselves in exactly such a situation as has been described--and the way you handle it may spell the difference between making and retaining friends among deaf people, and never getting to first base with them. It can also determine your future effectiveness in any work you may do with deaf people; between rapport with them, and resistance from them; between acceptance of your services and any help you may be able to provide them, and complete rejection of everything you represent, personally as well as professionally.

Deaf people have long memories--and, often, long tongues. An insult to one is soon known to many, via the efficient "deaf grapevine" of rumor--and the person who insults one deaf person in the way just described soon begins to encounter inexplicable reserve among deaf people--those with whom he has previously enjoyed a good relationship, as well as those he has never met before--all without knowing why. And, like all gossip, the facts fed into the "deaf grapevine" become distorted and magnified in the retelling. . . . Therefore, even if you are trapped in an unwilling conversation with a crashing bore who just happens to be a deaf person, and welcome the interruption like manna from heaven, DO observe the rules of common courtesy by apologizing for any interruption, and excuse yourself before you make your escape.

One might wonder at this point why deaf people are so sensitive about such matters as being treated with politeness and consideration by people who can hear, especially when one learns that deaf people are often apparently extremely rude to each other as well as to hearing people. A sociologist would perhaps attempt to explain this by drawing an analogy between the deaf subculture and those of other minority groups such as black people. A parallel can be drawn in some respects, but not in others. Black people know that some white bigots think they are an inferior race--but the black people themselves know they are not. Deaf people also know that some hearing people consider them to be inferior--but, differing from black people, deaf people often suspect that maybe the hearing people are right. Where black people, depending upon the degree of militancy with which they view the white race, regard manifestations of respect, courtesy, and consideration as confirmation of their own knowledge of the equality of their own race to that of the whites, and only what they feel is their due, deaf people regard such manifestations as offers of friendship, and indications that the hearing person can be trusted and depended upon not to kick the props out from under their fragile self-esteem.

Several research studies have shown that deaf people do suffer from very fragile egos. Their self-image is low, for they have been unintentionally conditioned since childhood to feel that they are inferior to normal children. Parents and teachers chatter away among themselves without regard for the child with straining eyes who is trying to catch what they are saying by watching their lips. In addition, they frequently discuss him in his presence--a fact of which he instantly becomes aware when he sees a hand casually brought up to the mouth so that his lipreading ability is defeated; or when the lip movements become deliberately small or stiff, and thereby hard to read; or when the head is ever so casually turned away from him so that he cannot see the lips; or when any of the small subterfuges hearing adults practice are employed in a blithe assumption that the deaf child will not know he is under discussion among those who control his destiny. Unfortunately, he does know, for he will have learned at a very early age what it means when a hearing person in his environment attempts to interfere with his ability to see the lips and read them, just as a hearing child learns very young that when adults resort to spelling out words, or to whispering--or even to various types of "codes"--that the topic under discussion is not meant for his ears, and egotistically, perhaps, he decides he is the topic of the conversation any time this happens.

A hearing child can fight back. He can develop rabbit ears which enable him to understand a whispered conversation from another room. He can learn the "codes." He will eventually learn to understand even spelled-out words. And, eventually, he finds out that such sotto voce conversations do not always concern him.

The deaf child, on the other hand, cannot fight his way to understanding. Not only is his lipreading ability all too often inadequate to the task of understanding grown-up conversation, but the subterfuges employed to further impede his ability to lipread by blocking or obscuring his sight of the lips are almost always successful. In addition, the one word he will most often recognize on the lips is his own name--and the few times he sees his own name filtering through the impediments thrown up to screen the conversation between his elders just serves to reinforce his belief that he is always the topic of conversation between hearing people any time he sees a hand move up to scratch a nose, a face turned momentarily away from his as the owner's attention is attracted by something on the other side of the room, or lip movements become different as the speaker's mood changes (and so is planted the seed of later suspicion of conversations between hearing people which seems so "paranoid" to those who deal with them as adults). Along with the feeling of inadequacy inherent in being "different" from normal children, the deaf child develops a concept of self which reflects his perceptions of how others perceive him--an individual "programmed for failure"--with decisions always made for him by hearing adults without his knowledge, and without his opinions being sought. It is easy to see why many of them eventually develop strong feelings of inadequacy which persist throughout their lives, for they interpret the activities of their elders as indicative of opinions that the deaf child/person is not capable of participating in any decision making about his own life--opinions they soon begin to share--and which, nine times out of ten, they carry over into adulthood even though experience may show that they are, indeed, capable of controlling their own destinies. They remain buried in their unconscious, to emerge any time a situation occurs which triggers those latent memories of being "excluded-because-of-incompetence."

To be sure, the deaf person learns in time that he is not always the topic of conversation between two hearing people who black him out by shifting from manual to verbal communication. In time, also, he becomes somewhat philosophical about unintentional rudeness in cases where the conversational blackout occurs when two hearing people, one or both of whom lack manual communication skills, start conversing with each other and unwittingly exclude him from understanding. But, in the case of those who could keep him in the conversation but do not take the trouble to do so, a deep, underlying resentment comes to the surface and colors both his reactions to the exclusion, and his perception of the situation as it pertains to himself. He feels unimportant, rejected--and suspects that the exclusion may be deliberate so that they could discuss him. A sophisticated, verbal deaf person may recognize his own reactions as immature, and know that his resentment is clouding his judgment, and call the oversight to the attention of the careless ones. But the majority of deaf people will simply withdraw into themselves, and cross off the names of the erring ones from their lists of hearing people they feel comfortable around.

The above rules can be summarized as:

1. Do keep your face and hands toward the deaf person with whom you are speaking.

2. Do maintain eye contact with the deaf person with whom you are conversing. He has to keep his eyes on you all of the time you are speaking--and expects you to do the same when he is talking to you whether verbally or manually.

3. Do not cover up your lips or face with your hands, or turn away from deaf persons present when talking with other hearing people. This applies to deaf children as well as deaf adults. If you must discuss a deaf person (child or adult) with another hearing person, do so at a time when the deaf person is not present. Leave the room if necessary--just as you would if a hearing child/adult were to be discussed--or wait for a time when he can be discussed in private.

4. Do not allow your attention to be diverted by another hearing person and engage in a verbal conversation with that person in the presence of the deaf person with whom you had been conversing until interrupted without at least apologizing for the interruption.

5. Do make every attempt to include any deaf person present in any conversation you are having with another hearing person. If you have manual skills, use them. If the other person also can use manual communication methods, the fact that you are using yours will often remind him to use his, and if it does not, you can subtly increase the likelihood of his remembering by interpreting his remarks to the deaf person. If he cannot use manual methods of communication, ask the deaf person if he has understood the other hearing person's remarks, and if he has not, tell him what was said.

6. Do not treat the deaf person like a child or a cretin. His language deficiency and/or lack of sophistication may cover up an excellent mind--his I.Q. may be much higher than yours-- and if you treat him like a half-wit, he will treat you with subtle contempt. So, grant him the dignity and respect due a normal person of the same age.

There are other more technical rules, those dealing with the mechanics of the language of signs, and the nature of the handicap rather than psychological or sociological aspects:

1. To get a deaf person's attention, a gentle tap on the shoulder or arm is best. The foot can be stomped if the floor is wooden and/or carries vibrations--or the hand rapped on the table--but care should be taken not to make the stomping and/or rapping too vigorous or sudden, for many deaf people are "spooky" in the sense that an unexpected loud vibration makes them jump. Turning the lights on and off is also an effective attention-getter.

   Note: Drumming fingers and tapping feet can drive a deaf person up a wall, as can kicking his chair, and so on. In addition, stomping the feet or slapping a table to emphasize a conversational point is sure to net you the attention of every deaf person within vibration range, so, unless you are intent on attracting their attention (or bugging them), it is best to control these tendencies toward drumming, tapping, stomping, pounding, or any such vibration-causing mannerisms when around deaf people.

2. In fingerspelling, the palm always faces forward except for G, H, J, P, and Q.

3. Unless otherwise specified (or in the case of a left-handed person), in any sign involving movement of one hand while the other remains still or makes smaller gestures, the right hand always does the moving or makes the larger gesture.

4. Fingerspelling is generally done by the right hand alone (or the left hand alone in the case of the left-handed person). One should avoid fingerspelling with first one hand and then the other unless this is done to make a distinct separation between two objects, two radically different one-word concepts, and so forth. (The latter technique is seldom used except by expert users of manual communication.)

I'll Be Doggoned's:

There are many things about the language of signs which often inspire the reaction of "I'll be doggoned!" from the beginner. In some cases, it is a rueful exclamation, as when the beginner finds that one sign can mean anywhere from three to eight or nine different words (for example, NEED, MUST, HAVE TO, NECESSARY, OUGHT TO, SHOULD) are all signed alike; or the reverse, where one word can be signed over a hundred different ways depending upon the context in which it is used (for example, RUN for a bus, RUN for the presidency, and so on). In other cases, it is an exclamation loaded with surprise and admiration when the student finds that a single sign can express far better than words a whole range of emotions depending upon the amount and type of emphasis, the facial expression, and the speed at which it is delivered; for example, FOR: What for? (a child whining); What the blazes did you do that for ??? (angrily); What's that for? (curiosity); etc. And, when one takes a single sign, such as LOOK, and shows all the various ways in which the basic, two-fingered LOOK sign can be used, the reaction is one of "Well, I'll be utterly doggoned!" at the versatility of the language of signs. All of the following concepts can be expressed merely by employing one or two hands, in the basic V-hand position, and moving them around to give a graphic picture of what the eyes are doing and seeing (your instructor can probably demonstrate them all):

1. Instructor looking at individual students in the class.

2. Individual students looking back at the instructor.

3. All students collectively looking at the instructor.

4. Instructor looking around the class, at students, at the room, at something over to the left or right of himself, etc.

5. Instructor "looking back" at the past events of his life.

6. Instructor looking forward to future events.

7. Instructor standing on top of a hill and looking at the view.

8. A wife, whose husband is being the "life of the party" glaring at him.

9. The husband's too-casual avoidance of her glare.

10. Eyes meeting across a crowded room--a boy and a girl, strangers to each other--neither of which wants the other to know that he/she is staring.

11. The eyes of a boy giving the once-over to a pretty, curvaceous girl.

12. A double-take, then a stare.

13. The eyes of a woman causally shopping down a store aisle, or window-shopping.

14. The eyes while hunting intently for something or someone.

15. A snub in which the eyes are deliberately averted.

16. A contemptuous up-and-down appraisal of someone guilty of a social faux pas.

17. The contemptuous look directed toward the speaker himself.

18. The mutually startled looks of two women who discover themselves wearing the same dress at a big social shindig, the hasty averting of their eyes, then the covert looks sneaked at each other to assess how well they look in the dress compared with the other person's appearance.

19. The raised eyeballs and "Oh my gosh" look of someone who has just discovered an exasperating error committed by someone else.

20. The examining of each other's faces, hair, eyes, lips indulged in by two people deeply in love who are cuddled together on a sofa.

21. The big-eyed stare of a little boy who meets his football hero in person.

22. The bored, patient look of a person who is forced to endure a long-winded chronicle of another person's surgery.

23. The surreptitious glances of a practical joker who is trying to keep a prospective victim from knowing he is being watched for his reaction when the trap snaps shut.

24. The quickly darting eyes of a professional thief casing a joint with a view toward thievery, and his eyes during the theft.

25. The innocent stare of a cheating husband when his wife accuses him of stepping out on her.

26. The puzzled glances students give each other when the instructor signs a test sentence they didn't quite understand.

27. The commanding "Look at that!" of a mother who finds a broken vase, etc.

LOOK is just one sign among many which can be used in this way. As you have probably begun to suspect after watching the ways in which one basic hand-position can be used to illustrate the moods and concepts inherent in any of two dozen different situations, facial expression, body movements, and the amount of emphasis one places on a given sign--as well as the speed with which the sign is executed--all play a vital role in conveying mood. One might say that the aforementioned factors take the place of tone and inflection in _speech_, and like tone and inflection in speech, are vital to the conveyance of meaning as well as mood. If one were to imagine speech in which there was no tonal inflection, no voice modulation, no emphasis, no pauses--just a monotone in which all words sound the same--then one begins to understand what expression, emphasis, and speed mean to the language of signs. They give it meaning, mood, and _life_.

Note: There are, however, limits to the amount of facial expression, bodily movements, and emphasis one should place upon one's signing. Just as an extremely loud voice, exaggerated variations in tone and inflection, and overdramatic vocalization in an ordinary conversation is jarring and unpleasant to the ear, so overexaggerated mugging, violent gestures, and too much emphasis are inappropriate to the language of signs unless called for by the context of the conversation or story. One should strive for the optimum--just enough expression, emphasis, and speed to suggest clearly the mood the speaker is trying to convey, and no more.

Another "Don't" is: don't get upset when you find that there are regional variations in given signs which confuse you the first few (or several) times you attempt to communicate with a deaf person in the language of signs. These are more or less the "dialectical" variations you would normally hear in the language spoken in different parts of the country, and will soon cease to throw you once you learn to concentrate upon the deaf person's message (and his lips) rather than on individual signs. Your instructor will, insofar as is possible, teach all the acceptable variations he knows for any given sign so that you can recognize them when you encounter them; but he may require that you learn to use the signs he, himself, uses. While the person doing the signing has a choice in which sign among several possible variations he will use, he has no control over the sign the other party will use--therefore he should learn to recognize all of the acceptable variations even if he does not use them in his own signing. The signs which are described in the word-descriptions you will be given in this course are, for the most part, those used by students at Gallaudet College in Washington, D.C., for Gallaudet has long acted as a "melting pot" in that students from all parts of the country congregate, exchange, adopt, and adapt signs among themselves, and then return to their home communities and disseminate their modified sign language among deaf people in their areas.

Also, do not become discouraged when you find you have trouble at first in reading what the deaf person is saying. Developing receptive skills is the roughest part of learning manual communication, and this is the reason why your instructor will be giving so many comprehension tests, drilling you so hard in receptive fingerspelling, and insisting that you use the language of signs with your fellow students as much as you can. After the first few times, you should gradually begin to be able to understand most of what your deaf friends say, even if it takes a while before you are able to read the fast-moving hands of two or more deaf people talking among themselves.

Do practice at home. While your instructor can help you tremendously in developing your receptive or reading skills, in the final analysis the responsibility for developing your ability to express yourself in the language of signs, your expressive skills, will rest upon your own shoulders. Your instructor can show you the signs, teach you how to execute them correctly; remedy any errors in technique you may make; teach you how to use them in various ways to express different meanings and moods; and see that you are exposed to them many times in the classroom. Unfortunately, he cannot help you practice each and every one of the hundreds of signs you will learn in this course enough times so that you will be able to remember them instantly and automatically when you need them. That part is up to you, and no one else. Therefore, overlearn your signs--try to use each one at least ten to twenty times in a variety of sentences--and you will "own" the sign in the sense that you will not forget it. If you do this, as your vocabularies of signs increase, you will soon find yourself "thinking" in sign language, a phenomenon which marks the end of the preliminary bumbling stage of the raw beginner, and the beginning of the development of fluency in the beautiful, picturesque, funny--and always interesting--Language of Signs.

Good luck!

THE MANUAL ALPHABET

FINGERSPELLING LESSON

The manual alphabet, or fingerspelling, is the pictographic representation of each of the twenty-six letters of the alphabet by twenty-six
different handshapes. Just as combinations of the twenty-six letters of
the alphabet are used to spell out words in the English language, so different combinations of the twenty-six individual handshapes of the manual
alphabet are used to fingerspell words. In essence, fingerspelling is
"writing in air," and can be used to give exact, verbatim translations of
English into visual, manual language. Unlike the language of signs, which
is ideographic in the main, fingerspelling is an exact transliteration of
English words into fingerspelled words by means of a sequential series of
handshapes, each of which represents the same letters in the same sequence
as they appear in the written words.

For the beginner, learning to fingerspell is not too difficult. What
is difficult is learning to <u>read</u> fingerspelled words on the hands of another person, for this skill entails the development of the <u>visual sequen-
tial learning</u> ability far beyond that required for reading the printed
word. In reading the printed word, one learns early to attend to the con-
figuration--the total appearance--of words, and then one's visual span begins to encompass clauses, phrases, and sometimes even sentences, without
the need to attend to the exact sequence in which the letters of the words/
clauses/phrases appear. In reading the fingerspelled word on the other
hand, only one letter at a time is visible on the hand, and a different
orientation must be developed if the beginner is not to fall into the trap
of attempting to identify each individual letter as it appears, then mentally trying to arrange the individual letters into a meaningful word.
Where the eye has only to identify a static, nonmoving pattern of letters
in the printed word, the eye must be trained in identifying patterns of
<u>movement</u> in order to identify the fingerspelled word; to attend to small
cues within the rapidly changing pattern, such as the position of the thumb
and the fingernails; the direction in which the fingers and palm point or
face; the number of fingers which are visibly extended from the fist, and
their relation to each other; and, finally, the tiny and sometimes almost
imperceptible differences between the respective heights of curved and
straight fingers.

Despite the difficulty all beginners experience in learning to read
fingerspelling, it is a task which must be successfully accomplished, as
is that of learning to fingerspell one's own words clearly and fluently.
The reason for this is simple: there are hundreds of thousands of words
in the English language--and only a few thousand formal signs. Those countless words for which no signs exist can only be conveyed through finger-

spelling, or communication with deaf people will be inadequate and restricted. One might say with considerable justification that the manual
alphabet is the basic foundation stone of the language of signs, for it
can be adequate by itself as a means of communicating with deaf people,
whereas signs alone are not.

If the student masters fingerspelling, then his learning of manual
communication is facilitated, for as he increases his vocabulary of signs,
he can substitute signs for words he formerly fingerspelled while continuing to fingerspell those words for which he has not yet learned the
signs, or for which no signs exist. Without the ability to fingerspell,
he would have to wait until he had a vocabulary of several hundred signs
before he could carry on even a limited conversation with a deaf person,
whereas fingerspelling gives him an immediately utilizable skill he can
employ as soon as he has learned the twenty-six handshapes of the manual
alphabet. In addition, each sign he learns thereafter adds to the flexi-
bility of his communication ability, and speeds up his delivery of a message. By the same token, he is immediately able to receive messages from
deaf persons--even if he requires a very slow rate of fingerspelling and
many repetitions at first.

Fingerspelling, therefore, is of primary importance to any student in
manual communication, and the beginner should bend every effort toward
mastering this basic skill.

There are a few cardinal rules in fingerspelling which the student
should learn and follow. First and foremost is the rule that the hand
should be positioned so that the palm faces toward the person being addressed (except for the letters G, H, P, and Q--and to an extent, J).
Second, the hand should be aligned on a vertical-horizontal plane which,
if imaginary lines were drawn from the middle fingertip to the elbow, and
across the hand at the junction of the fingers with the palm (palm knuckles), an exact cross would be formed in which the vertical bar is at a
90 degree angle to the floor, and the horizontal bar of which is exactly
parallel to the floor. This is most easily accomplished by dropping the
arm to a natural position at one's side, then, leaving the elbow where
it normally would fall, bringing the hand up to a position in front of
the shoulder of the side the fingerspelling hand is on. This also positions the hand in the best place for both the lips and the fingerspelling
hand to be seen at the same time, for most deaf persons focus their eyes
upon the face of the person talking to them, and catch the fingerspelling
and signs with their peripheral vision.

Another cardinal rule is: spell clearly. In other words, do not try
to sacrifice clarity in the interests of speed. Speed in fingerspelling
comes naturally as a consequence of practice, and the student who forces
himself to spell faster than is comfortable is likely to develop faulty
habits of delivery which detract from the clarity of his fingerspelling.

A third rule, which has been mentioned previously but cannot be over-
emphasized is: Say the complete word you are fingerspelling, not the

individual letters of the word! Discipline yourself to practice constantly until you can master this essential task, for the habit of alphabetizing during fingerspelling is one of the most annoying among bad habits a person can develop in manual communication--and the most difficult to break once it becomes established. As was mentioned earlier, deaf people concentrate upon a speaker's face--primarily his lips--so that they can use whatever lipreading skills they have to reinforce what they are getting from the signs and fingerspelling, and there are few more disconcerting and confusing faults a person can have than that of alphabetizing a fingerspelled word, for the deaf person (often one of limited language ability) must then mentally sort out the collection of individually mouthed or spoken letters and then try to arrange them into a meaningful word. To exemplify this, imagine yourself trying to understand a speaker who says, "Tee aitch ee pee ess eye cee aitch oe ell oe gee wye oe eff tee aitch ee dee ee aye eff," instead of "The psychology of the deaf." Not only does it slow one down, but it utterly baffles the deaf person and forces him to look at your hand instead of your lips if he is to understand you--and often disconcerts him to the point where he misses the next couple of signs which follow the fingerspelled word, because he is busy trying to remember the letters you spelled, and trying to arrange them into a word he can understand.

Preliminary Lessons 1 and 2 are designed to help you practice what you will learn in class, but should not be considered to be the sum total of the training you will need in fingerspelling--your instructor will not end your training in fingerspelling until the end of the entire course, and you should continue your self-training and practice throughout the course as well. As you practice, you will develop fluency, and as you develop fluency, you will develop speed. And your instructor will bend every effort to train you in reading fingerspelling if you cooperate with him by doing your part. Between the two of you, and your classmates as well, you should be fairly competent at both expressing yourself in fingerspelling, and in reading it on the hand of another person by the time the course ends.

THE MANUAL ALPHABET, A TO L
(FRONT VIEW)

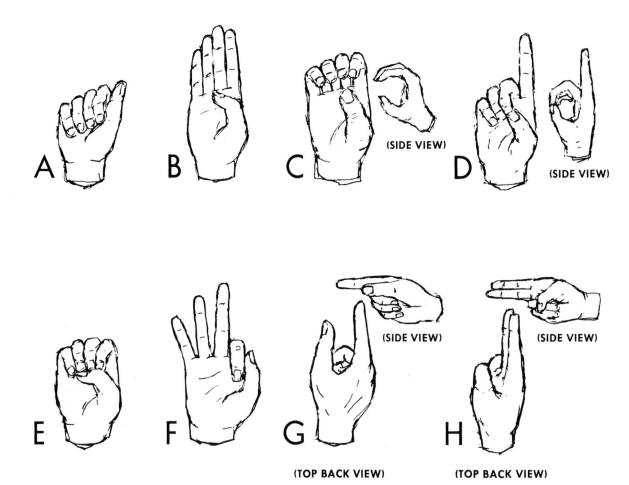

A

B

C (SIDE VIEW)

D (SIDE VIEW)

E

F

G (SIDE VIEW) (TOP BACK VIEW)

H (SIDE VIEW) (TOP BACK VIEW)

I

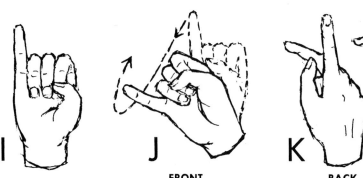

J
FRONT
(THREE-QUARTER VIEW)

K
BACK
(THREE-QUARTER VIEW)
(SIDE VIEW)

L

THE MANUAL ALPHABET, M TO Z
(FRONT VIEW)

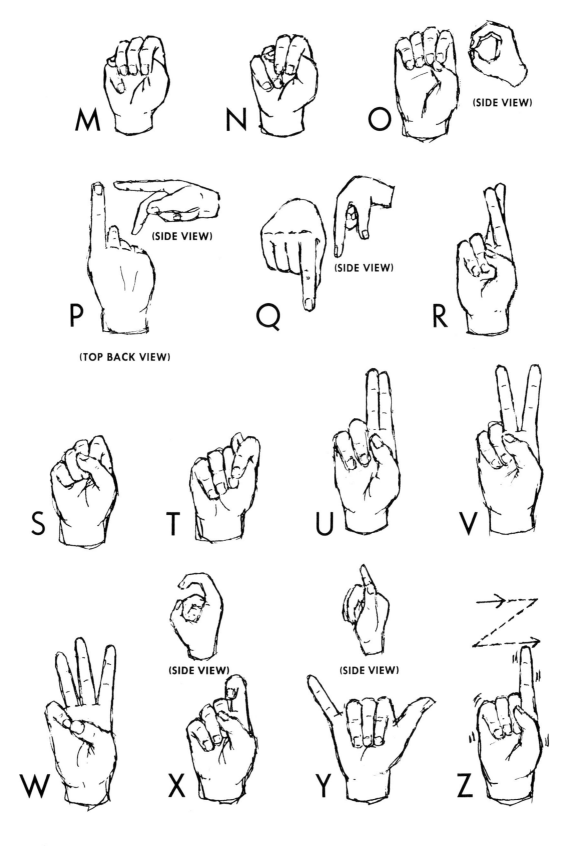

M

N

O (SIDE VIEW)

P (SIDE VIEW)

(TOP BACK VIEW)

Q (SIDE VIEW)

R

S

T

U

V

W

X (SIDE VIEW)

Y (SIDE VIEW)

Z

PRACTICE WORDS AND SENTENCES IN FINGERSPELLING

A to N

Cab	Bleak	Beamed	Deflea	Lick
Cabbie	Flaked	Backed	Lacking	Knack
Bedded	Kicking	Named	Macie	Fleck
Faded	Jabbed	Liking	Jake	Flicked
Deaf	Clammed	Biking	Jim	Fallen
Dean	Calming	Hiking	Jamb	Needing
Abel	Hedged	Clinging	Leaning	Heeding
Able	Man	Mane	Cleaned	And
Enable	Meaning	Image	Clacked	Hand
Faded	Declined	Glide	Blacken	Banded
Facile	Jamming	Gadding	Blackening	Manned
Defamed	Clanking	Aga	Ham	Maned
Indeed	Jibbed	Again	Heeded	Becalmed
Magic	Bleeding	Gained	Jill	Babe
Blend	Necking	Faced	Jibe	Damage
Blending	Blended	Flea	Kicked	If
				Had

A to Z

Adz	Each	None	Zebra	Learn
Fan	Man	Purple	Were	Thank
Map	Life	Queer	Pink	Come
Law	Way	Rested	Home	Done
Box	Red	Union	Sister	Quit
Jar	Hear	Velvet	Uncle	Sign
Sky	Rock	Winter	Apple	Since
Hat	Wife	Yearly	Black	Trying
Mat	Kiss	Flirt	Mine	Tomorrow
Cow	Green	Jealous	Grasp	Experience
Job	Lace	Excel	Ideal	School
You	Last	Family	Open	Explain
Bat	With	Coax	Quill	Understand
Aero	And	Snow	Glove	Maybe
Want	Bank	Where	Teach	Stinker
Dare	Cold	Twins		

Practice Sentences (Fingerspelling)

1. The quick brown fox jumps over the lazy dog.
2. Now is the time for all good men to come to the aid of their party.
3. Peter Piper picked a peck of pickled peppers.
4. Quit exaggerating, you crazy creep!
5. We will learn signs in the next lesson.

**PART I: BEGINNING SECTION:
THE LANGUAGE OF SIGNS**

LESSON 1

THE LANGUAGE OF SIGNS

The word-descriptions of the signs in each lesson in this manual are
based on certain handshapes, or <u>hand-positions</u> (as they are called in
this book). The hand-positions are illustrated and described in the pages
which follow this introduction, and, in order for the student to follow
the word-descriptions, he must learn the hand-positions thoroughly. If
he does not, he will <u>not</u> be able to understand precisely how a sign is
executed from reading the word-description.

<u>To use word-descriptions</u>. To avoid making more work for himself than
is necessary, the student should follow a standard sequence of steps in
figuring out what the word-description is telling him to do with his hands.
First of all, he should read the instructions for the <u>hand-position</u> of the
hand (or of each hand if both are used in the sign). Until he reads the
instructions for <u>palm-direction</u>, he should assume that the hand is positioned (relative to his body) in the normal fingerspelling position; that
is the <u>palm</u> of the hand will face the person being addressed, with the
thumb on the inside and the little finger on the outside, and the fingertips (of the hand when opened) or the palm knuckles (of closed hand) pointing toward the ceiling. If the instructions direct that the palm face
<u>left</u>, <u>right</u>, or <u>self</u> the student should then turn his hand so that the palm
faces the required direction, keeping fingertips (of open hand) or palm
knuckles (of closed hand) pointing toward ceiling. If the instructions
direct the student to have his palms facing the <u>ceiling</u> or the <u>floor</u>, he
should <u>not</u> attempt to accomplish this by bending his hand at <u>the wrist</u>, but
should drop his <u>forearm</u> (keeping his wrist straight) until the angle formed
by upper and lower arm is approximately 90 degrees before turning his palm
in the required direction.

Once the student has his hands in the correct hand-position, and his
palms facing in the required direction, he should then attend to whether
or not there are <u>additional</u> instructions with regard to the direction in
which the fingertips or palm knuckles should be pointing. If there are
none, the student can safely assume that he has his hands in the correct
<u>beginning</u> position of the sign, and can proceed to follow the directions
for movement of the hand(s) or arms. If there are additional directions
for fingertip or palm knuckle positioning, the student will have to move
his hands and/or forearms until he has both palm direction and finger/
knuckle alignment correct. This is far from as complicated as it may seem
from reading the foregoing, for, as the student reads the word-descriptions,
he will find that most signs make use of the <u>natural</u> alignment of human
fingers, hands, palms, wrists, and arms, and do <u>not</u> require any straining
of muscles or awkwardness of juxtapositioning in order to align the hands

32

correctly. (A good rule of thumb to follow is: If it feels <u>awkward</u>, you are doing it <u>wrong</u>.)

While the foregoing may offer the student help in using the <u>word-descriptions to refresh his memory about how a sign is executed</u>, and to perfect his understanding of the exact handshapes and motions required, it must be reiterated that the word-descriptions should not be used to <u>learn</u> signs which have not yet been demonstrated, because all signs have certain little idiosyncracies which cannot effectively be described in words or pictures, but which can be demonstrated easily and instantly by the skilled instructor. Just as one cannot learn to speak fluent, unaccented, idiomatic French from a <u>textbook</u>, neither can one learn to use manual communication fluently from books, or pictures, or even movies. In the final analysis, if one wants to learn to communicate with people by using a specific method of communication, be it a foreign language or the language of signs, the best way to learn the method is by learning from a native of that language, or from one who is as fluent as a native. Manual communication is not a written language one can read. It is a form of communication between human beings just as spoken language is, and it should be learned in the same way it will be used--from human beings skilled in this form of communication--not from books, pictures, or word-descriptions.

GENERAL INSTRUCTIONS FOR COMPLETING
HOMEWORK ASSIGNMENTS

1. Regular "recital" sentence assignments:

These sentences are those your instructor will require you to compose and practice for recital purposes in the classroom. They
should be kept current, whether you use them or not in reciting in
the classroom, and this means writing new sentences for each lesson
as your vocabulary of signs increases. After composing the sentences, you should practice each one until you can do each of them
smoothly and with a minimum of hesitation, for the instructor may
call upon you to demonstrate them in front of the class at any given
time. Not only will they afford you the opportunity to demonstrate
your increasing ability in manual communication, but they will also
provide your fellow students with additional training in the receptive skills, for they will be required to "read" what you signed and
fingerspelled, as well as offer you constructive criticism on your
performance.

In composing recital sentences, you should endeavor to use as many
words as possible from those for which you have already learned
the signs. Fingerspell those words for which you have not yet
learned the signs (or for which no signs exist), but concentrate
on using as many of the signs you know as possible. These sentences need not be turned in to your instructor unless he requests
that you do so. But, keep them current, and practice them each
time you compose them, whether the instructor calls upon you to
demonstrate them or not!

2. "Cloze" sentence assignments:

These sentences are in addition to the recital sentences, and, like
the recital sentences, should be constructed in such a way that as
many of the words as possible should be those for which you have
already learned the signs. However, Cloze sentences differ in one
important respect from recital sentences, for they must include a
word for which you will be taught the sign in the next class session, and must be constructed in such a way that the sentence context provides clues as to what the sign to be taught actually means.
They will be used in a special type of learning drill by your instructor, and this means that they must be turned in to your instructor at the beginning of the class session immediately following the
one in which the assignment was made.

What your instructor will do is sign and fingerspell the Cloze sentences, using the sign to be taught without telling the class what
the sign means. The students will be required to figure out from
the context of the sentence what the unknown sign means, for they

will know (or should know) what all of the other signs and finger-spelled words were. For example, suppose the current month is March. The Cloze sentence most likely to elicit the meaning of the sign for MONTH would be something like:

"Next _____ will be April."
(MONTH)

You will find at the end of each lesson in this manual a page upon which are printed the words for which signs will be taught in the next lesson. Your instructor will divide these words up among you and your fellow students and require that each of you write up to three Cloze-type sentences using the words you have been assigned. You should circle the ones you have been assigned, and, unless your instructor directs otherwise, you can assume that any words preced-ing your assigned words on the list will have been taught by the time the instructor reaches you and your sentences. This will assist you in composing your sentences. (However, your instructor may not want to go to the trouble of arranging the homework papers in sequen-tial order before teaching the signs on the list, so it is best that you check with him before assuming that the signs for the words pre-ceding yours on the list will have been taught before the instructor uses your homework in the drill.)

3. Outside assignments (in Appendix):

These assignments are self-explanatory and designed to help you acquire experience in using your newly developed skills with "real live" deaf people, as well as to gain some awareness of what is going on in your local community of deaf people. Your instructor will give any additional information or instructions at the time the assignments are given.

position
placement
movement.

HAND POSITIONS

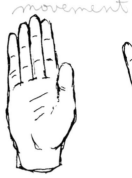

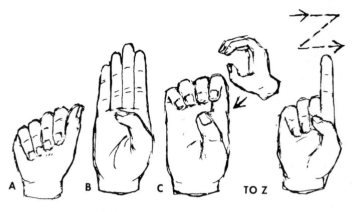

1. OPEN-HAND (FINGERS-CLOSED)

2. 5-HAND

A   B   C   TO Z

3. "ALPHABET" HANDS

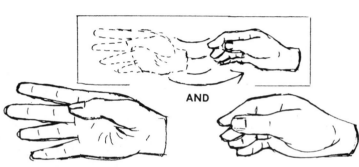

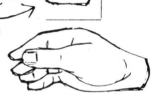

AND

4. OPEN-HAND

5. AND-HAND

6. INDEX-HAND

7. RIGHT-ANGLE INDEX HAND

8. RIGHT-ANGLE HAND

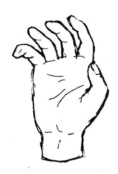

9. CUPPED-HAND

10. CLAWED-HAND

11. TOUCH-HAND

EXPLANATION OF HAND-POSITIONS

1. Open-hand (Fingers-closed): In this position, the hand is open, palm flat, and fingers and thumb all are together.

2. 5-hand (also called Open-hand, Fingers-spread): In this, the hand is open, palm flat, and fingers and thumb all are separated as when one indicates the numeral "Five."

3. Alphabet-hand: In this position, the hand forms whichever manual letter the "hand" calls for; that is, an A-hand means a hand in position indicating the manual letter "A."

4. Open-and hand: This position is the one the hand assumes at the beginning of the sign AND.

5. And-hand: This position is the one the hand assumes at the end of the sign AND.

6. Index-hand: In this position, the hand assumes the configuration it does when one wants to indicate the numeral, "one" (the thumb should be across the fingers remaining against the palm, not alongside the index finger nor extended away from the palm).

7. Right-angle index hand: Similar to index-hand, except that the index finger is bent at the palm to form a right angle with the palm (from the palm to the tip, however, the index finger remains straight, not bent or hooked).

8. Right-angle hand: In this position, the fingers of an open-hand bend at the palm to form a right angle with the palm, the fingers, themselves, remaining straight from the palm knuckles outward. The thumb is placed against the second knuckle of the index finger, not extended nor placed against the palm.

9. Cupped-hand: In this, the open-hand is slightly bent at the palm (fingers remain straight from palm outward) and the tip of the thumb is aligned with (and placed against) the second knuckle of the index finger, thus forming a little hollow in the palm of the hand.

10. Clawed-hand: In this, the fingers and thumb of the 5-hand are all curved and hooked to make a clawlike hand. If one pretends to grip a large softball, one will have the correct configuration.

11. Touch-hand (basic configuration for all affective, sensing and emotion-conveying signs): In this, the hand is spread in the 5-hand position, but, the middle finger only is dropped slightly toward the palm. The other fingers and thumb remain extended as in 5-hand position.

WORD-DESCRIPTIONS OF SIGNS IN LESSON 1 VOCABULARY

Note: The student will find it helpful to remember that there are certain basic hand-positions and movements which are used in combination to indicate specific personal pronouns, and whether the pronoun is singular or plural. These are described below in summary form for quick reference purposes. For more detailed descriptions see the word-description of the sign for each pronoun.

Key Hand-Positions (or handshapes):

Index-hand: Used for all personal pronouns used as subject or object except for I, WE, and US (described in detail below).

Open-hand, fingers-closed, palm flat: Used for all possessive forms of personal pronouns except OUR (in which the palm is cupped, not flat).

A-hand: Used for all pronouns ending in -self or -selves (reflexives).

Key Hand and Arm Movements:

Hand makes single movement ending on center of own chest: All first-person-singular pronouns.

Hand moves straight toward person being addressed: All second-person-singular pronouns.

Hand describes semicircle directly in front of center of body: All second-person-plural pronouns.

Hand makes a straight, single movement to one side (or the other) of center front: All third-person-singular pronouns.

Hand describes semicircle, beginning and ending off to the left (or right) of center front: All third-person-plural pronouns.

Hand begins sign on one shoulder and, describing semicircle in front of chest, ends at other shoulder: All first-person-plural pronouns.

1. I: I-hand, palm toward left, thumb touching chest.

2. ME: Right angle index-hand, finger pointing toward and touching chest.

3. MY: Open-hand, fingers-closed, palm flat, placed on chest, palm to chest.

4. MINE: Same as MY.

5. <u>MYSELF</u>: <u>A-hand</u>, palm to left, knuckles to ceiling, bump thumb against chest twice.

6. <u>YOU (singular)</u>: With <u>index-hand</u>, palm to floor, point at the person being addressed.

7. <u>YOU (plural)</u>: Similar to YOU, except that hand describes a semicircle from left to right (or the reverse) to point at several people instead of a single person, with the center of the semicircle being directly in front of the signer.

8. <u>YOUR (singular)</u>: With <u>open-hand, fingers-closed</u>, palm forward, push hand a few inches toward person being addressed. Do NOT use to mean YOU'RE!!

9. <u>YOUR (plural)</u>: Similar to YOUR (singular) except that hand describes a semicircle to encompass several people instead of just one (like in YOU (plural)). Do NOT use to mean YOU'RE!!

10. <u>YOURSELF</u>: With hand in <u>A-hand</u> position, palm to left and thumb on top (and slightly extended), push hand <u>twice</u>, rapidly, a few inches toward person being addressed.

11. <u>YOURSELVES</u>: (a) Similar to YOURSELF except that hand describes semicircle to encompass a group instead of pushing twice at one individual.

     (b) Similar to YOURSELVES except that hand pushes once toward each of several individuals in a group. (Used when it is desired that particular emphasis be placed on individuals within a group, rather than the group as a whole.)

12. <u>HE, HIM, SHE, HER</u>: (Usually fingerspelled when the words begin a sentence, or if there is a need to discriminate between two or more persons, or between two persons of different sexes. <u>Always</u> fingerspelled when the person being discussed is first mentioned in a sentence or conversation.)

     (a) Point at the person and then fingerspell HE or SHE as the case may be.

     (b) Point at the person being discussed, if present.

     (c) If a person being discussed is not present, it ordinarily suffices to use the colloquial sign--A-hand, palm to self, thumb to right and extended, jerk hand to the right in a brief gesture-- similar to the common gesture used by hearing people to pantomime "Get a load of him!"

40

13. <u>HIS, HERS</u>: Similar to YOUR (singular) except that the hand pushes toward the person being discussed if present. If person is not present, the hand pushes off to the right (or left) of center rather than toward person(s) being addressed.

14. <u>HIMSELF, HERSELF</u>: Similar to YOURSELF except that the hand is pushed twice toward the person being discussed (if present). If person is not present, the same sign as for YOURSELF is used, but the hand pushes twice to the left (or the right) of center instead of directly at the person or persons being addressed.

15. <u>IT</u>: (a) If an object, point to it.

   (b) If used as an indefinite "it," fingerspell.

16. <u>ITS</u>: Same as for HIS or HERS. (Possessive form only as in, "I sent the dog to ITS bed." <u>Do not use</u> for the contraction "it is.")

17. <u>THEY, THEM</u>: Similar to YOU (plural) except that the semicircle described by the hand is positioned to the left (or to the right) of center, with the semicircle beginning to the left (or right) of center, and continuing even further to the left (or right). Note: The "Get a load of him (them)" gesture can also be used, but thumb should describe small, horizontal semicircle from front to rear to encompass more than a single "he" or "she."

18. <u>THEIR</u>: Similar to YOUR (plural) except that the semicircle is off to one side as described in THEY, THEM.

19. <u>THEMSELVES</u>: Similar to YOURSELVES (a) and (b), except that the semicircle is off to one side as previously described for THEY, THEM, and THEIR.

<u>Note</u>: In all the following <u>first-person-plural</u> signs, the following movement from right shoulder to left shoulder (for a right-handed person) is the basic movement of the sign, with only hand-positions changing according to the word being signed: The right hand, palm to left, touches the thumb side of the hand to the <u>front of the right shoulder</u>, then describes a semicircle in front of the chest, the hand rotating so that the movement ends with the <u>little finger</u> edge of the hand against the front of the <u>left shoulder</u>.

20. <u>WE, US</u>: (a) Indicate both words with <u>index-hand</u> performing the shoulder-to-shoulder movement described above.

   (b) For WE, use <u>W-hand</u> instead of <u>index-hand</u>, and for US, use <u>U-hand</u>, in both cases, performing the movement described above.

21. <u>OUR, OURS</u>: Perform movement described above with hand in <u>cupped-hand</u> position. (Some people prefer to use an <u>O-hand</u>, but most people still use the <u>cupped-hand</u>.)

22. OURSELVES: Perform movement described above, using an A-hand, thumb
    edge of hand against right shoulder and slightly extended. How-
    ever, do not rotate hand so that the sign ends with the little
    finger edge of the hand against the left shoulder--simply touch
    the thumb edge of the hand to both shoulders.

23. WHAT: (a) Natural sign. Both hands in 5-hand position, palms to
    ceiling, in universal gesture of helplessness.

    (b) Left hand, in 5-hand position, palm to ceiling. Draw
    index finger of right hand across fingers of left hand from in-
    dex finger to little finger, like running a stick along a picket
    fence.

24. HOW: Both hands in A-hand position, palms to floor, index finger
    knuckles touching. By turning both your wrists, simultaneously,
    roll the second knuckles of each hand together (or rock them
    back and forth quickly and briefly).

25. PRACTICE: Left hand in index-hand position, palms to self, index
    fingertip pointing to right; right hand in A-hand position, palm
    to floor, and knuckles pointing forward. "Polish" index finger
    of left hand with the flat "bottom" of the right fist by brushing
    back and forth from fingertip to last knuckle.

26. THINK: Bring tip of index finger of right-angle-index-hand, palm to
    self, up to and touch temple.

27. KNOW: Right-angle-hand, palm to self, bring fingertips up to touch
    temple.

28. DON'T KNOW: Sign KNOW then, in an abrupt "flicking water off the
    fingertips" gesture, snap hand around to palm forward 5-hand
    position.

29. CONFUSED: Sign THINK, then follow by both hands in clawed-hand posi-
    tions, palms toward each other, slightly separated. Twist wrists
    in a "mayonnaise-jar-opening" motion to indicate metal gears get-
    ting out of synchronization.

30. NOT: (a) A-hand, palm to left, ball of thumb touching under part of
    chin, bring forward a few inches in front of chin.

    (b) Both hands in open-hand, fingers-closed position, palms
    forward and flat, cross and then uncross wrists so that hands end
    up side by side four or five inches apart. (Usually used in place
    of DO NOT, whereas NOT (a) is used as indefinite NOT, ISN'T, etc.)

31. UNDERSTAND: O-hand, thumb touching temple. Snap index finger up into
    the air, other fingers remaining in position.

42

32. <u>NO</u>: Fingerspell U, O quickly, snapping fingers and thumb together.

33. <u>YES</u>: Right hand in <u>A-</u>, <u>S-</u>, or <u>Y-hand</u> position (all are acceptable), palm forward and knuckles to ceiling. Nod hand from the wrist (keeping arm stationary) like a head nods on the neck.

34. <u>HELLO</u>: Right hand in <u>open-hand, fingers-closed</u> position. Bring to forehead in a "saluting" gesture, then move hand forward a few inches.

35. <u>GOODBYE</u>: Natural gesture--wave the fingertips of the raised right hand in the universal "bye bye" gesture.

36. <u>QUESTION MARK SIGN</u>: With hand in <u>X-hand</u> position, wiggle index finger up and down rapidly.

37. <u>AND</u>: <u>Open-and-hand</u>, palm to left, thumb edge of hand uppermost, move hand quickly to the right a few inches, closing it to <u>and-hand</u>.

38. <u>RIGHT</u>: Both hands in <u>index-hand</u> position, index fingertip pointing forward. Begin sign with right hand directly above left hand, index fingers parallel and pointing forward, with hands separated about three inches, then bring right hand down briskly until it makes abrupt contact with the left hand. (Be careful with this sign. Remember, it is made with <u>INDEX-HANDS</u>, not <u>H-</u> or <u>V-hands</u>!)

39. <u>WRONG</u>: With right hand in <u>Y-hand</u> position, palm to self, thumb to right and little finger to left, rap second knuckles of middle three fingers against chin.

PRACTICE SENTENCES

Note: Add your recital sentences to the bottom of the list.

1. I love myself.

2. You should practice thinking for yourself.

3. We got ourselves into a lot of trouble.

4. All of you know what to do, don't you?

5. He said "Hello" to her. She snubbed him.

6. What are they doing?

7. I don't know her. Do you?

8. I am confused. I don't understand him.

9. Are your friends coming with us?

10. What do I do next?

11. I asked my mother, but she said "No."

12. It takes practice to understand signs.

13. The dog did not like its dinner.

14. How did you know I like cherry pie?

15. What is your address? I think I live near you.

16.

17.

18.

19.

20.

NOTES

Signs taught in Lesson 1:

1. I	14. Your (sing.)	27. Himself, herself
2. Me	15. Your (pl.)	28. It (a) and (b)
3. My, mine	16. Yourself	29. Its
4. Myself	17. Yourselves	30. They, them
5. You (sing.)	18. He, him; she, her	31. Their
6. You (pl.)	19. His, hers, her	32. Themselves
7. We, us (a) and (b)	20. Know	33. Hello
8. Our, ours	21. Don't know	34. Goodbye
9. Ourselves	22. Confused	35. Question mark
10. What (a) and (b)	23. Not (a) and (b)	sign (?)
11. How	24. Understand	36. And
12. Practice	25. No	37. Right
13. Think	26. Yes	38. Wrong

Additional signs learned in class, or additional usages of above signs:

Other notes (including additional homework assigned by instructor if any):

LESSON 2

WORD-DESCRIPTIONS OF SIGNS

1. DID YOU, DO YOU, ARE YOU, WERE YOU: Either ? (question mark sign) YOU, or fingerspell DID then sign YOU (substituting DO, ARE, or WERE as necessary). Most commonly used is the ? sign.

2. WILL, WOULD, FUTURE, NEXT: With right hand in 5-hand position, palm to left and fingertips to ceiling, touch thumb to angle of jaw then draw whole hand upward and forward about eight or nine inches out in front of the cheek. For FUTURE, extend the gesture further forward in two motions, the second motion being a spiral extension of the first.

3. WAS, PAST, AGO, BACK, BEFORE: (Note: BEFORE is signed like this only when the sentence is something like "I have been there before.")

    (a) Right hand in open-hand, fingers-closed position, palm to right shoulder. Move hand back over right shoulder (or tap balls of fingers to right shoulder).

    (b) Right hand in 5-hand position, palm facing left and fingertips to ceiling. Circle hand upward and backward until thumb rests against right shoulder.

4. A LONG TIME AGO: Similar to WAS, PAST, AGO, BACK, BEFORE (b) above except that hand describes larger circle, moves slower, and repeats the circle two or three times.

5. NOW: Both hands in either right-angle or Y-hand positions, palms to self. Drop hands slightly until palms are facing ceiling.

6. TODAY: Sign NOW, NOW rapidly. (Note: NOW is also used to indicate THIS in signs indicating the present time such as THIS MORNING, THIS AFTER-NOON, THIS EVENING; and TO- in TONIGHT. TODAY can also be signed an-other way, which will be described in Lesson 4 vocabulary.)

7. SAME, ALIKE: (a) Both hands in index-hand position, palms to floor and fingertips pointing forward. Bring hands together so both index fingers are parallel and touching along their full length.

    (b) Right hand in Y-hand position, palm to floor, knuckles facing forward. Move hand from left to right and back again twice (keeping hand in same hand-position, and making the movement from the elbow, not the wrist).

    (c) Like (b) above, except that both hands are used, and move in opposition to each other (that is, left hand moves to the right and

45

right hand moves to the left, then both hands reverse direction, etc.). However, this sign is commonly used to mean MATCH (or MATCHING) as well as SIMILAR.

8. DIFFERENT: Both hands in index-hand position, palms forward, and index fingers crossed at the second knuckle. Keeping hands in index-hand position, separate hands (uncross fingers), ending sign with both hands about twelve inches apart and parallel. (Important note: Use the elbow as the fulcrum for the movement.)

9. BUT: Identical to DIFFERENT above, except that the wrist is used as the fulcrum or pivot joint for the movement, and the hands end up about six inches apart.

10. ABOUT: Left hand in and-hand position, palm and fingertips pointing to the right; right hand in index-hand position (or right-angle index), palm to self. Circle tip of right index finger around fingertips of left hand.

11. AM, ARE, IS, BE: Note: Auxiliary verbs, if used at all by the signer, are usually fingerspelled. However, there are two ways--one old and one new--of signing some of them:

   (a) Right hand in index-hand position, palm to left and fingertip to ceiling. Touch thumb side of index finger to center of chin, then bring hand straight forward two or three inches (old sign which is sometimes used to indicate any of the above words). Used primarily in platform signing.

   (b) Using the same chin-out movement of the hand, substitute the following hand-positions for the index-hand required for the old sign:

   AM: A-hand
   ARE: R-hand
   IS: I-hand
   BE: B-hand

12. WAS, WERE (new signs): Similar to the new signs for AM, ARE, and so on, except that after the chin-out movement, the hand proceeds to sign PAST (described earlier). The hand-positions used are:

   WAS: W-hand
   WERE: R-hand

13. TO: Both hands in index-hand position; left hand palm to self, and right hand palm forward. Left hand remains stationary, about six inches in front of and to the left of right hand, while right hand moves forward until ball of right fingertip touches ball of left fingertip.

14. CALL (summon): Both hands in open-hand, fingers-closed position, palms to floor. Tap back of left hand with fingertips of right hand, then bring right hand back and upward, ending sign with right hand in A-hand

or <u>right-angle</u> hand-position in normal fingerspelling position in front of <u>right</u> shoulder.

15. <u>CALL (phone)</u>: With right hand in <u>Y-hand</u> position, bring hand to cheek in such a way that the thumb is in the position a telephone earpiece would be held, and the little finger is in the position of the telephone mouthpiece.

16. <u>NAME</u>: Both hands in <u>H-hand</u> position, fingertips forward and palms facing each other, place second knuckle of the middle finger of the right hand on the second knuckle of the index finger of the left hand so that the fingers of both hands make an X.

17. <u>CALL (as in "What are you called?")</u>: Sign NAME, but after fingers are crossed, move both hands forward about six inches (if the person being called/named is second or third person), or backward toward self (if the sentence is first person, such as "They call me Joe").

18. <u>INTRODUCE</u>: Similar to NAME above except that before the fingers are crossed in the NAME sign, they are held about twelve inches apart and then simultaneously describe downward curving arcs, coming back up to end in the sign for NAME.

19. <u>DUMB, STUPID, IGNORANT</u>: (a) Right hand in <u>A-hand</u> position, palm to self. Knock knuckles against forehead.

    (b) Right hand in <u>V-hand</u> position, palm forward. Bring hand backward and knock the knuckles joining fingers and palm against forehead.

20. <u>WORD</u>: Left hand in <u>index-hand</u> position, palm to right and fingertip to ceiling; right hand in <u>G-hand</u> position, palm facing left hand. Touch tips of right index finger and thumb to <u>top third</u> of left index finger. (Referent here is to part of a slug of type printers make on linotype machines.)

21. <u>SIGN</u>: Both hands in <u>index-hand</u> position, palms forward and fingertips angled toward ceiling. Circle the hands around each other, making the circles move <u>backward</u> and <u>downward</u> before going forward and upward (or <u>counterclockwise</u> when signer is viewed in profile from the right).

22. <u>LANGUAGE</u>: Both hands in <u>L-hand</u> position, palms forward and fingertips to ceiling. Touch thumbs to each other, then move hands slowly apart about eighteen inches, while simultaneously rocking both hands from side to side so that the thumbs point alternately toward the ceiling then toward each other (fingertips remain pointed forward).

23. <u>STORY, SENTENCE</u>: Similar to LANGUAGE above except that <u>F-hands</u> are used. However, SENTENCE is often followed by QUOTE, in which the hands are placed about eighteen inches apart, at shoulder height, both in <u>V-hand</u> position. The fingers of the V are then quickly bent to look like the quotes at the beginning and end of a sentence being quoted.

24. FINGERSPELLING: Right hand in 4-hand or 5-hand position, but bent at
     the palm (bent-4 or bent-5-hand position) so that the fingers remain
     straight but the hand is bent when viewed in profile. With palm and
     fingertips pointing forward, move the hand from left to right about
     six or eight inches while waving each of the fingers alternately up
     and down (keeping them straight) so that the fingertips describe a
     sort of rippling motion. (The thumb does not move.)

25. TELL, SAY, SAID: Right hand in index-hand position, palm to self, and
     fingernail of index finger against soft underside of chin. Draw hand
     straight forward to about six inches in front of chin. (Note: There
     are several variations of signs having to do with talking, conversing,
     speech, lectures, and the like, which your instructor will demonstrate.
     All are modifications of the sign described above, with slight varia-
     tions in hand-position or motion, and some use two hands instead of
     one, and so forth.)

26. DAYS OF THE WEEK: Signs for the days of the week from Monday through
     Saturday are all made with the hand in regular fingerspelling position
     in front of the shoulder, palm forward. The hand makes a small, clock-
     wise (from the signer's viewpoint) circling motion. The hand-positions
     used for each are:

     MONDAY: M-hand
     TUESDAY: T-hand
     WEDNESDAY: W-hand
     THURSDAY: H-hand
     FRIDAY: F-hand
     SATURDAY: S-hand

     SUNDAY: made with both hands in open-hand, fingers-closed position,
        palms forward and fingertips to ceiling. With hands about eighteen
        inches apart and held at shoulder height, push both hands forward
        simultaneously twice. (This is similar to the sign for WONDERFUL,
        although there are differences in the amount of emphasis used as
        well as slightly different movements. Your instructor will demon-
        strate these slight differences.)

PRACTICE SENTENCES

Note: Add your recital sentences to the bottom of the list.

1. Did you tell her about the phone call?

2. Today, I have to go to town.

3. What shall we do now?

4. She wore a different dress today.

5. At first, she said "No," but then she changed her mind about it.

6. Will you introduce me to your friend, please?

7. It was a long time ago, and I don't do that now.

8. Of all the stupid things to do, telling him about it takes the prize.

9. Will you call Jonny to dinner, please?

10. They both wore the same dress to the party.

11. My name is Marilyn, but they call me Lynn.

12. I didn't understand a word you said.

13. She came here on Monday, but left on Wednesday.

14. On Friday, we will have an exam.

15. Sign language is fun to learn.

16.

17.

18.

19.

20.

50

NOTES

Signs taught in Lesson 2:

1. Did you, do you, etc.
2. Was, past, last, ago, back, before (a) and (b)
3. A long time ago
4. Now
5. Today (a)
6. Same, alike (a), (b), and (c)
7. Different
8. But
9. About
10. Am, are, is, be (old and new)
11. Was, were (new)
12. To
13. Call (summon)
14. Name
15. Call (phone)
16. Call (named)
17. Introduce
18. Dumb, stupid, ignorant (a) and (b)
19. Word
20. Sign
21. Language
22. Story, sentence (quote)
23. Fingerspelling
24. Tell, say, said
25-31. Days of the week
32. Will, would, future, next

Additional signs learned in class, or additional usages of above signs:

Other notes (including additional homework assigned by instructor if any):

NUMBERS LESSON

WORD—DESCRIPTIONS OF SIGNS

1. NUMBER: Both hands in and-hand position, palms and fingertips facing each other. Touch fingertips of hands together twice, rotating hands in opposite directions (that is, left hand moves counterclockwise, and right hand moves clockwise when viewed from the right profile) slightly before touching fingertips the second time. (Also used to mean PUT TOGETHER, as in assembling something.)

2. MANY: (Either one or both hands can be used. Use both for emphasis.) Both hands in modified E-hand position (like E-hand except that the thumb covers the fingernails), palms to ceiling. Snap fingers of hands open to open-and position, then repeat quickly.

3. MUCH, ABOVE: Both hands in right-angle position, palms and fingertips facing each other. Place fingers of right hand on top of fingers of left hand, then raise right hand about four or five inches (left hand remaining stationary).

4. LESS: The reverse of MUCH, above, in that fingers of right hand are placed under the fingers of the left hand, then the right hand is lowered a few inches (left hand remaining stationary as before).

5. FEW: Right hand in A-hand position, palm to ceiling. One at a time (but rapidly), extend index finger, then middle finger, then third finger (keeping little finger in place with the thumb), using the thumb as a "brake" on each finger, until hand is in W-hand position.

6. SEVERAL: Like FEW above, except that little finger joins the other fingers in its turn, so that the hand ends up in a position in between 5-hand and open-and hand.

7. HOW MANY, HOW MUCH: Sign MANY, but raise the hand sharply while the fingers are opening, beginning the sign at about waist height, and ending it at about shoulder height. (Almost like you were throwing a ball up in the air.)

8. OLD: Right hand in C-hand, place thumb-edge of hand against chin, with palm to left. Close hand to S-hand and lower it as if gripping a beard and pulling it downward.

9. HOW OLD: Sign OLD, then HOW MUCH.

10. MORE: Both hands in and-hand position, palms and fingertips facing each other. Touch fingertips together twice, rapidly.

11. THAN: Both hands in B-hand position, palms to floor. (Right hand's fingertips point forward, left hand's fingertips point toward right front.) With fingers of right hand a few inches above left fingertips, drop right hand below left hand quickly, striking fingertips of left hand with edge of right index finger in passing.

51

NUMBERS

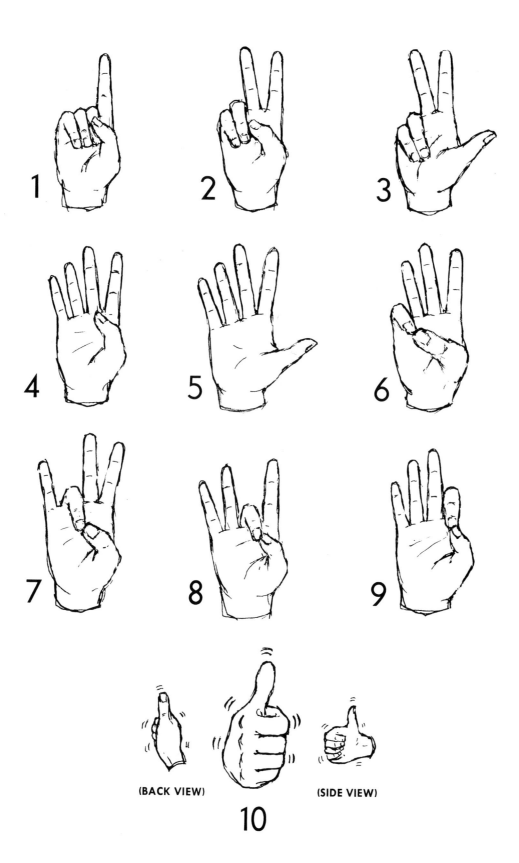

1

2

3

4

5

6

7

8

9

(BACK VIEW)   (SIDE VIEW)

10

DIRECTIONS FOR SIGNING NUMBERS

Direction of Palm

1 . . . 5	Palm faces toward yourself (with certain exceptions your instructor will explain).
6 . . . 9	Palm faces forward.
10 . . . 15	Palm faces toward self again.
16 . . . 19	A-hand, with palm to self, then palm forward with the number.
20s	Except for 22, begin with L-hand, palm forward: 22 is the "oddball" number of the 20s.
30s, 40s, 50s, etc.	Palm always forward: hand always makes a slight sidewise motion while in the first number, then changes to the hand-position of the second number.
100s	Palm always forward: Spell 1C, 2C, and so on, snapping the fingers up into the C-position.
1000s	Spell 1, 2, 3 (or whatever), palm forward, then place right M-hand in center of palm of other hand: or spell 12C, 14C (for 1,200, 1,400, etc.)
1,000,000	Spell 1, 2, 3 (etc.), palm forward, then place right M-hand in center of palm of other hand, lift it up again (a couple of inches), then replace it in palm a few inches forward of the position in which you placed it the first time.

Helpful Hints:

1. When giving a date, the name of the month is usually fingerspelled, but abbreviated (except for months with short names—March, April, May, June, and July) exactly as it is abbreviated in writing. February therefore becomes Feb., August becomes Aug., and so on.

2. When stating a time, the left wrist is tapped once, then the time is given exactly as spoken. 8:30, therefore, becomes (tap wrist) 8, 30 (not 8, 3, 0).

NUMBERS FOR PRACTICE

7	1,456	April 11, 1965
9	3,430	June 13, 1962
8	4,587	August 29, 1925
3	6,902	September 30, 1943
10	1,786	December 7, 1941
5	2,345	October 31, 1901
14	1980	November 4, 1934
19	1942	January 20, 1932
24	1492	January 1, 1966
21	1964	February 14, 1962
67	1932	April 16, 1941
98	1957	March 25, 1867
37	1961	April 12, 1945
41	$.01	August 14, 1943
62	$.05	May 30, 1984
76	$.10	March 7, 1916
86	$.15	December 8, 1914
90	$.25	May 15, 1917
16	$.20	January 13, 1976
11	$.75	February 28, 1966
23	$1.00	July 4, 1965
124	$1.50	June 27, 1942
160	$.57	July 24, 1776
240	$2.89	November 27, 1964
342	$3.98	January 30, 1965
458	$4.00	February 8, 1932
679	$25.00	Today, the _____
		(use the date this
		list is distributed)

Practice Sentences Using Numbers

1. I'll see you around 8:00 tonight.
2. He is in his early fifties.
3. They live at 21453 South Main Street.
4. Our new color TV cost us $755.59.
5. You can't buy liquor if you're under 21.
6. In 1492, Columbus sailed the oceans blue.
7. In November, 1970, we had a very heavy snow.
8. There were 1,349 people at the ball.
9. About 1,300 people were killed in the quake in Iran.
10. It costs $.39 at Safeway, but $.27 at I.G.A.

NOTES

Signs taught in numbers lesson:

1.	Number	7.	How many, how much
2.	Many	8.	Old
3.	Much, above	9.	How old
4.	Less	10.	More
5.	Few	11.	Than
6.	Several		

Additional signs learned in class, or additional usages of above signs:

Other notes (including additional homework assigned by instructor if any):

LESSON 3

WORD-DESCRIPTIONS OF SIGNS

1. GOOD: Right hand in open-hand, fingers-closed position, palm to body.
   Touch fingertips to lips or chin, then push hand forward and slightly
   downward. Similar to THANK sign. (For more emphasis, place back of
   right hand in the palm of left hand at end of sign.)

2. FINE: Right 5-hand, palm to left. Touch thumb to chest, then move hand
   forward a few inches in a fast, happy gesture.

3. BAD: Right hand in open-hand, fingers-closed position, palm to self and
   fingertips toward ceiling. Place fingertips on chin, and in a sharp,
   choppy gesture, rotate hand so palm faces outward (and is alongside
   face), then slap it sharply downward so that fingertips end up pointing toward floor.

4. LOUSY: Right hand in 3-hand position, palm to left and thumb on nose
   (with fingertips pointing to ceiling). Arc hand from thumb-on-nose
   position sideways and upward (to a position alongside and a little bit
   to the front of the face), then slap sharply downward as in BAD. (Note:
   Hand remains in 3-hand position throughout.)

5. NO GOOD: Fingerspell NG, moving hand several inches sideways between the
   N and the G in a snapping motion.

6. THANK (YOU): Sign GOOD, but drop the hand farther and extend it slightly
   forward.

7. EXCUSE (ME): Left open-hand, fingers-closed, palm to ceiling and fingertips to right front. Right hand in right-angle hand, palm toward
   floor. Wipe fingertips of right hand across palm of left hand twice,
   moving from heel of palm toward palm knuckles. (Then sign ME.)

8. VERY: Both hands in V-hand position, fingertips forward and palms facing
   each other. Touch fingertips of V-hand fingers together, being careful
   not to touch thumbs or palms together, then separate fingertips a couple
   of inches.

9. SORRY: Place right A-hand, palm toward body, on center of upper chest
   and move in a circular motion.

10. PLEASE: (Also means ENJOY, and some deaf use this sign to mean LIKE.)
    Right hand in open-hand, fingers-closed position, palm flat against
    the chest, rubbed in a circular motion.

11. CAN: Both A-hands, palms to floor. Drop slightly.

12. ABILITY: Sign CAN, CAN, CAN (also used to denote POSSIBLE or POSSIBLY, and occasionally for OPPORTUNITY and/or CHANCE).

13. THIS: Left hand in open-hand, fingers-closed position, palm facing ceiling and fingertips toward right front; right hand in Y-hand position, palm toward floor. Place right hand in center of left palm. (Also used to mean THAT in some contexts.)

14. THIS (time concept): In such usages as "this morning," "this evening," "at this time," etc., THIS is signed exactly like NOW (see Lesson 2).

15. THAT: (a) Sign like THIS (above). Used for emphasis, or as an indefinite article.

    (b) Right hand in Y-hand position, palm facing the object being identified, push hand toward object a few inches.

16. TIME: Tap index finger of right hand on back of left wrist (natural gesture).

17. DAY: Left arm (palm flat and toward floor) straight across waist. Place elbow of right arm on left fingertips. Right arm at right angle to left arm. Right D-hand and arm describe semicircle in front of face and body from right to left, right elbow remaining on left fingertips. (This is not as complicated as it looks on paper.)

18. ALL DAY: Both hands in open-hand, fingers-closed position; left hand palm down, with arm held across the waist. Placing right elbow on back of left hand, and using right elbow as the pivot (or fulcrum), describe an arc of almost 180 degrees from right to left with the right forearm and hand, beginning the sign with the right hand palm up and to the extreme right, and ending it with the right hand palm down and almost touching the left elbow.

19. MORNING: Left hand open-hand, fingers-closed; right hand cupped-hand. Put fingers of left hand midway between wrist and right elbow. Right hand extended forward, palm up.

20. NOON: Same right angle arms as DAY, save that right hand is a B-hand, not D-hand, and remains stationary to indicate the sun is directly overhead.

21. AFTERNOON: Both hands in open-hand, fingers-closed position; left hand in same position as described for ALL DAY; right elbow on back of left hand, palm toward floor and hand held about eight to twelve inches in front of and above left forearm, pat right hand downward a few inches twice.

22. NIGHT: (a) With both hands in right-angle position, palms to floor, place right wrist on top of back of left hand.

    (b) Both hands in open-hand, fingers-closed position, palms facing self, drop both toward each other, crossing and stopping almost parallel. Signifies darkness--pulling the curtains. (Platform usage only.)

23. EVENING: Similar to NIGHT (above) except that right hand is raised (with right forearm remaining against back of left hand) so that fingertips point forward instead of toward floor.

24. ALL NIGHT: Similar to ALL DAY (described earlier) except that the 180 degree arc described by the right forearm and hand travels downward (below the horizon formed by the left forearm and hand), and the right hand begins the sign palm downward and ends it palm toward ceiling.

25. ALL DAY AND ALL NIGHT: (Can also be used for DAY AND NIGHT.) Sign ALL DAY, then ALL NIGHT, without inserting AND, and keeping the motion continuous.

26. MIDNIGHT: Is signed almost exactly like NOON, except that the right hand and arm are pointed directly at the floor.

27. YESTERDAY: Right A-hand, palm to left. Touch thumb to front part of cheek then to back part of cheek near ear. (Can use Y-hand also.)

28. TOMORROW: Right A-hand, palm to left. Touch ball of thumb to cheek, then move hand forward a few inches pivoting hand so that sign ends with hand, palm to body, thumb pointing to ceiling. (Hand remains in A-hand position throughout.)

29. DO, ACT, BEHAVE: Both hands in C-hand position, palms to floor. Move both hands away from each other a few inches then back toward each other. Repeat.

30. CAN'T, CANNOT: Both hands in index-hand position, palms to floor. Begin sign with right hand about six inches above left hand, then drop right hand to about six inches below left hand, with right index finger striking left index finger as it drops.

PRACTICE SENTENCES

Note: Add your recital sentences to the bottom of the list.

1. Good afternoon, how are you?

2. That is a very bad excuse. In fact, it is a lousy excuse.

3. This time tomorrow, we will know many new signs.

4. How old were you when you knew right from wrong?

5. Many of us didn't understand what he was talking about.

6. It took more money than I had.

7. In 1776, the Declaration of Independence was signed.

8. How many of you know the story?

9. I was very sorry to have missed her.

10. I spent all day and part of the evening practicing for the play.

11. The ability to read fingerspelling comes with practice.

12. Several of my friends told me about what a good voice you have.

13. Please excuse me, I'm very sorry.

14. Jimmy has been feeling lousy, but feels good now.

15. We watched TV last night until midnight.

16.

17.

18.

19.

20.

PRACTICE SENTENCES

TO DO, ACT, BEHAVE

The verbs underlined are usually fingerspelled. The question-mark (?) sign can be substituted for all "do" verbs, however. The verbs capitalized are all signed DO. (Some instructors may prefer that you substitute the "new" signs for the TO BE auxiliary verbs.)

1. What <u>do</u> you DO on Sundays?

2. What <u>does</u> your father DO on Saturday?

3. What <u>was</u> the boy DOING?

4. What <u>will</u> you DO tomorrow?

5. What can I DO to help you?

6. I don't care what you DO. You, yourself, DO what you decide.

7. Why <u>did</u> you want to DO that?

8. What must I DO next? or (What <u>do</u> I have to DO next?)

9. What have you DONE with my book?

10. What time <u>do</u> you have to DO your homework?

11. Mary DID all the work alone. Why didn't you help her DO it?

12. I have DONE all the work you told me to DO.

13. Bob won't DO his work.

14. Mrs. Brown <u>is</u> DOING much good for her church.

The verbs ACT, PERFORM, and BEHAVE are also signed DO.

1. Many children ACTED nicely. One boy ACTED silly.

2. Jane's dog ACTS sick. She will take him to the doctor.

BEHAVE and PERFORM are also signed as DO.

1. The pupils BEHAVED well when the teacher was away.

2. The deaf actors PERFORMED very well in the "The Cat and the Canary."

HOMEWORK ASSIGNMENT

"CLOZE" SENTENCES

Words for which signs will be taught in Lesson 4

 1. Help
 2. Must
 3. Get
 4. Have
 5. Work
 6. Job
 7. Necessary, have to, ought to, should, need
 8. No (none)
 9. Experience
10. Expert
11. Again
12. Slow
13. For
14. Learn
15. --er sign
16. Student
17. Teach
18. Teacher
19. School
20. College
21. University
22. High school
23. Minute, second
24. Hour
25. Later, afterwhile
26. Week
27. Next week
28. Month
29. Next month
30. Year
31. Next year
32. Last week
33. Last month
34. Last year
35. Last night
36. Today (b)
37. This morning
38. This afternoon
39. This evening
40. One month ago
41. Two years from now
42. ___ years from now, etc.

1. Circle the words for which you have been assigned to write sentences.

2. Write your sentences on a separate sheet and turn it in to your instructor at the beginning of the next class session.

NOTES

Signs taught in Lesson 3:

1. Good	11. Can	21. Noon
2. Fine	12. Can't	22. Afternoon
3. Bad	13. Ability	23. Night
4. Lousy	14. This	24. Evening
5. No good	15. This (time concept)	25. All night
6. Thank (you)		26. Day and night
7. Excuse (me)	16. That (a) and (b)	27. Midnight
8. Very	17. Time	28. Yesterday
9. Sorry	18. Day	29. Tomorrow
10. Please	19. All day	30. Do, act, behave
	20. Morning	

Additional signs learned in class, or additional usages of above signs:

Other notes (including additional homework assigned by instructor, if any):

LESSON 4

WORD-DESCRIPTIONS OF SIGNS

1. <u>HELP</u>: Right hand, palm flat and toward ceiling. Left <u>A-hand</u> placed on center of right palm and both hands raised slightly.

2. <u>MUST</u>: <u>X-hand</u>, palm to floor, drop a few inches.

3. <u>GET</u>: Relaxed <u>C-hands</u>, palms facing each other but right hand above left hand (reverse if southpaw), separated by a few inches. Close hands to <u>S-hands</u> rapidly, bringing hands together so that right <u>S-hand</u> is on top of and touching left <u>S-hand</u>, right little finger to left thumb.

4. <u>HAVE</u> (possessive): Both <u>right-angle</u> hands, palms to body. Bring fingertips to chest, separated by about six inches.

5. <u>WORK</u>: Both <u>A-hands</u>, palms to floor. Cross wrists with right hand on top. Brush right upper wrist forward a couple of times across back of left wrist.

6. <u>JOB</u>: Same as WORK.

7. <u>NECESSARY, HAVE TO, NEED, SHOULD, OUGHT TO</u>: All signed MUST.

8. <u>NO</u> (as in "I have no job."): Both hands in <u>0-hand</u> position, palms facing each other and separated by about six inches. Push hands toward audience a few inches, separating them by about twelve inches. (Just one hand can also be used.)

9. <u>EXPERIENCE</u>: <u>Open-and hand</u> (fingers straight instead of curved). Place thumb and fingertips at temple. Draw hand outward an inch or so, closing fingers and thumb meanwhile, ending up with <u>and-hand</u> a few inches from head.

10. <u>EXPERT, SKILL</u>: Left hand, palm flat, fingers closed, palm to right. Cup right hand along outer (little finger) edge of left palm, closing hand around it. Then move right hand downward, closing hand to <u>A-hand</u>, palm forward. (Left hand does <u>not</u> move.)

11. <u>AGAIN</u>: Left hand, palm flat and facing ceiling. Right <u>right-angle</u> hand, palm to ceiling, is turned over, palm to floor and fingertips in center of left palm.

64

12. SLOW: Left hand, palm flat and facing floor. Right hand, palm flat but relaxed. Fingertips of right hand are drawn slowly along back of left hand and wrist from fingertips back to wrist and arm. (Note: Hands should be almost parallel.)

13. FOR: Sign THINK, then move hand a few inches from the forehead, turning it so that it is palm forward, fingertip to ceiling. (You will often see a deaf person saying--"for for." This is deaf "idiom" for WHAT FOR.)

14. LEARN: Left hand in open-hand, fingers-closed position, palm to ceiling and fingertips to right front. Right hand in open-and hand, fingers-closed position. Place right fingertips against left palm, then lift it upward and backward until the back of the right hand is at the forehead, meanwhile closing hand to and-hand position. (Some deaf people do this twice, but do not bring the hand all the way to the forehead. They also use this for STUDENT.)

15. -ER SIGN (agent sign): With both hands in open-hand, fingers-closed position, about twelve inches apart, palms toward each other and fingertips forward, place the heels of both palms against the sides of the chest and move them down to the waistline. (This is the "person" sign. For example, WORKER would be signed WORK, then ER. BAKER would be signed COOK, then ER, and so on.)

16. STUDENT: Sign LEARN, then -ER.

17. TEACH: Both hands in and-hand position, palms and fingertips forward. Both hands begin the sign in a position about level with your eyes and about a foot apart. Push both hands forward at the same time. Do this twice, rapidly.

18. TEACHER: Sign TEACH, then sign -ER.

19. SCHOOL: Clap both hands twice. (Denotes teacher clapping her hands for attention.)

20. COLLEGE: Start sign in same position as for SCHOOL, then sweep the right hand up in a circular motion to a position about six inches above left palm, keeping palms parallel to each other.

21. UNIVERSITY: Sign COLLEGE, and while right hand is circling above left hand, change the hand-position to U-hand, palm forward and fingertips to ceiling.

22. HIGH SCHOOL: Fingerspell HS fast (mouthing the words "high school"), moving the hand quickly sideways about four inches while the hand is changing from H to S.

23. MINUTE, SECOND: Left hand in open-hand, fingers-closed position, palm to right and fingertips to ceiling. Right hand in index-hand position, palm to left. Place heel of right hand against palm of left hand, with fingertip pointing to ceiling. Move index finger of right hand about a half-inch clockwise (toward left little finger).

24. HOUR: Position hands as for MINUTE, but have right index hand describe full clockwise circle around left palm, keeping index fingertip toward ceiling.

25. AFTERWHILE, LATER: Position hands as for MINUTE, then turn right index hand clockwise to the right (right fingertips point first to ceiling, then end up pointing forward). Left hand remains stationary. Do this rapidly twice. (You can place thumb of right hand against center of left palm while doing this.)

26. WEEK: Left hand in open-hand, fingers-closed position, palm to right and fingertips pointing to right front. Right hand in index-hand position, fingertip pointing to ceiling, palms facing each other. Place heel of right hand against heel of left palm and slide right hand across left palm from heel of hand toward fingertips.

27. NEXT WEEK: Sign WEEK, then slide right index hand off end of left hand and move it forward a few inches. Do this in a circular motion so that right index hand ends up a few inches above and directly over left hand.

28. MONTH: Both hands in index-hand position. Left hand palm to right, fingertip to ceiling. Right hand palm to self, fingertip to left. Place back of right index finger against side of left fingertip and draw it downward toward wrist.

29. NEXT MONTH: Sign WILL, then MONTH.

30. YEAR: Both hands in S-hand position, palms to self and knuckles facing each other. Place right hand above left hand, then circle it forward, downward, back, and place it again in position on top of left hand. Right fist, in other words, circles around left fist.

31. NEXT YEAR: Can be signed FUTURE, then YEAR, or you can use the more common one that follows: Both hands in S-hand position, palms to self and knuckles facing each other as in YEAR. Place right hand on top of left, then while left hand remains stationary, right hand changes to index-hand position and moves forward, fingertip pointing forward.

32. LAST WEEK: Sign WEEK PAST.

33. LAST MONTH: Sign PAST MONTH.

34. LAST YEAR: Both hands in <u>S-hand</u> position. Place right fist on top
    of left fist, then with right hand in <u>index-hand</u> position, palm to
    self and fingertip to ceiling, "throw" your index finger back over
    your shoulder, or point it back over your shoulder. Left <u>S-hand</u>
    remains stationary.

35. <u>LAST NIGHT</u>: Sign YESTERDAY NIGHT.

36. <u>TODAY</u>: (Often signed just NOW, NOW.) Sign NOW DAY.

37. <u>THIS MORNING</u>: Sign NOW MORNING.

38. <u>THIS AFTERNOON</u>: Sign NOW AFTERNOON.

39. <u>THIS EVENING</u>: Sign NOW EVENING.

40. <u>ONE MONTH AGO</u>: Sign MONTH, then follow directions for last part of
    LAST YEAR, with index finger "thrown" back over shoulder.

41. <u>TWO YEARS AGO</u> (up to five years ago): Follow directions for LAST YEAR,
    but "throw" the number of fingers over your shoulder as there are
    years you want to indicate.

42. <u>TWO (UP TO 5) YEARS FROM NOW</u>: Follow directions for "S" type of NEXT
    YEAR, but right hand, after hitting left fist, changes into <u>2-hand</u>
    or <u>3-hand</u> according to number of years you want to indicate. Then
    move right hand forward.

PRACTICE SENTENCES

Note: Add your recital sentences to the bottom of the list.

1. You must have experience if you are to get a job.

2. We worked all day yesterday and far into the night.

3. It isn't necessary for you to come back.

4. Did he tell you about his new job?

5. It helps to have an expert show you how to do it.

6. Will you say that again, slowly, please? I didn't understand you.

7. She had no thought for anyone but herself.

8. You must learn to think for yourself.

9. Our teacher is very experienced.

10. That will teach you not to be so slow!

11. I graduated from high school in 1958.

12. He said he would see us afterwhile.

13. It takes years to become an expert in sign language.

14. Did you go to college?

15. I have been offered a job for next year.

16.

17.

18.

19.

20.

HOMEWORK ASSIGNMENT

"CLOZE" SENTENCES

Words for which signs will be taught in Lesson 5

1. Male
2. Female
3. Man
4. Woman
5. Child
6. Baby
7. Boy
8. Girl
9. Gentlemen
10. Lady
11. Father
12. Mother
13. Son
14. Daughter
15. Sister
16. Brother
17. Marry, wed
18. Husband
19. Wife
20. Which
21. When (specific)
22. When (during, while)
23. Book
24. Read
25. Study
26. Write
27. Pencil, pen
28. Type, typewriter
29. Secretary
30. Lesson
31. Paper
32. Print
33. Often
34. Sometimes
35. Always
36. Never

1. Circle the words for which you have been assigned to write sentences.

2. Write sentences on a separate sheet and turn it in to your instructor at the beginning of the next class session.

NOTES

Signs taught in Lesson 4:

1.	Help	15.	--er sign	29.	Next month
2.	Must	16.	Student	30.	Year
3.	Get	17.	Teach	31.	Next year
4.	Have	18.	Teacher	32.	Last week
5.	Work	19.	School	33.	Last month
6.	Job	20.	College	34.	Last year
7.	Necessary, etc.	21.	University	35.	Last night
8.	No (none)	22.	High school	36.	Today (b)
9.	Experience	23.	Minute, second	37.	This morning
10.	Expert	24.	Hour	38.	This afternoon
11.	Again	25.	Later, afterwhile	39.	This evening
12.	Slow	26.	Week	40.	One month ago
13.	For	27.	Next week	41.	Two years ago
14.	Learn	28.	Month	42.	___ years from now, etc.

Additional signs learned in class, or additional usages of above signs:

Other notes (including additional homework assigned by instructor, if any):

LESSON 5

WORD-DESCRIPTIONS OF SIGNS

1. MALE: (The basic position for all signs denoting male gender. Derived
    from the hand holding the brim of a hat.) Right hand in open-and
    hand, closing to and-hand as the hand "takes hold of a hat brim."

2. FEMALE: The basic position for all female signs. A-hand. Move the
    ball of your thumb across your cheeks from each toward mouth. (De-
    rived from the days of the bonnet ribbons women used to have crossing
    their cheeks.)

3. MAN: Sign MALE, then measure a height taller than yourself with a right-
    angle hand. (The sign described for MALE is often used with and-hand
    pushed forward about four inches to indicate MAN. Shortcut method.)

4. WOMAN: Sign FEMALE, then measure height taller than yourself with right-
    angle hand.

5. CHILD: Right-angle hand. Measure a height considerably smaller than
    yourself. For CHILDREN, do this twice more, moving hand to the right
    as you measure out each child.

6. BABY: Natural sign--cradle a baby in your arms.

7. BOY: Same as MAN, only measure a height smaller than yourself or make
    MALE sign twice, quickly.

8. GIRL: Sign FEMALE twice, rapidly, or sign FEMALE then measure height
    considerably shorter than yourself with right-angle hand.

9. GENTLEMAN: Sign MALE, then FINE.

10. LADY: Sign FEMALE, then FINE (often used for WOMAN, too).

11. FATHER: Right hand in A-hand position, palm to left. Place thumb on
    forehead, then open hand quickly to 5-hand.

12. MOTHER: Same as for FATHER except that thumb is placed on chin instead
    of forehead.

13. SON: Sign MALE, then BABY.

14. DAUGHTER: Sign FEMALE, then BABY.

15. SISTER: Sign FEMALE, then ALIKE.

16. BROTHER: Sign MALE, then ALIKE.

17. MARRY, WED: Clasp hands, right hand on top of left, palm to palm.

18. HUSBAND: Sign MALE, then MARRY.

19. WIFE: Sign FEMALE, then MARRY.

20. WHICH: Both hands in A-hand position, palms facing each other but separated by a couple of inches. Move each hand up and down alternately.

21. WHEN (specific): Both hands in index-hand position. Left hand palm upward, or facing the body, remains stationary. Right hand describes a circle with its fingertip, palm away from the body, around the left finger then back until the right fingertip touches the left fingertip.

22. WHEN (during): Both hands in index-hand position, parallel, palms down. Move both forward a few inches, describing a slight, downward arc.

23. BOOK: Place both hands (in open-hand, fingers-closed position) in a "prayer" attitude, then, keeping the outside edges of the palms together, open the hands like a book.

24. READ: Left hand in open-hand, fingers-closed position, palm to self. Right hand in 2-hand position, palm to floor and fingertips to left palm. (This denotes the two eyes.) With fingertips pointing to left palm, move them back and forth as if reading a page of print printed on your left palm.

25. STUDY: Point the fingertips of right bent 4-hand at left palm and sign FINGERSPELL at the palm of your left hand.

26. WRITE: Natural sign. Using left palm as a piece of paper, "hold a pencil" in your right hand and "write" on your left palm.

27. PENCIL: Pretend to hold a pencil in your right hand. Bring it to your mouth as if moistening the tip, then sign WRITE.

28. TYPEWRITE: Natural sign. Pantomime typing on a typewriter.

29. SECRETARY: Pretend to remove a pencil from your ear, then sign WRITE. You may follow this with the -ER sign if you wish, but it is not necessary. This sign is sometimes made with U-hand instead of "pencil-gripping" hand. The U-hand touches the ear, then comes down and traces a line across the left palm.

30. <u>LESSON</u>: Left hand in <u>open-hand, fingers-closed</u> position, palm to self, fingertips to ceiling. Right hand in <u>right-angle</u> hand-position, palm to left, and knuckles to ceiling. Place outside edge of right hand against left palm fingertips, then lift it away a little bit and place it against left palm center. (Indicates a lesson covering the top of the page to the bottom.)

31. <u>PAPER</u>: Both hands in <u>open-hand, fingers-closed</u> position. Left hand palm upward, fingertips to right front. Right hand palm to floor, fingertips to left front. Brush right palm <u>backward</u> a couple of times against left palm, moving from fingertips to palm of left hand.

32. <u>PRINT</u>: Left hand <u>open-hand, fingers-closed</u>, palm to ceiling, fingertips forward. Right hand in <u>20-hand</u> position. Place thumb of right hand against left palm and make twenty, two or three times.

33. <u>OFTEN</u>: Left hand in <u>open-hand, fingers-closed</u> position, palm to ceiling. Right hand <u>right-angle</u> hand, palm to floor. Touch fingertips of right hand hand to left palm three times, moving fingertips from the base of the left palm to the fingertips.

34. <u>ONCE</u>: Left hand in <u>open-hand, fingers-closed</u> position, palm to ceiling. Right hand in <u>index-hand</u> position. Touch right fingertips to left palm, then hold up one finger, palm to body. For twice, use <u>V-hand</u> position and do the same. For thrice, use <u>3-hand</u> position and do the same.

35. <u>SOMETIMES</u>: Sign ONCE twice, quickly. (When SOMETIMES is signed very slowly, it means OCCASIONALLY or ONCE IN A WHILE.)

36. <u>ALWAYS</u>: Right <u>index-hand</u> position, palm to ceiling, describes a couple of largish circles in the air.

37. <u>NEVER</u>: Right <u>B-hand</u>, palm to left. Starting at about eye level, fingertips pointing forward, hand describes a large question mark in air. (The tail of the ? should go off to your <u>right</u> in a chopping motion.)

PRACTICE SENTENCES

MUST, NEED, HAVE TO, SHOULD, OUGHT TO, NECESSARY

Note: All words underlined in each sentence are indicated by the single
        sign for MUST. (Do not add the sign for TO.)

1.   The children have to return to school on Sunday afternoon.

2.   I must have more money before I can buy a new car.

3.   The boy must learn to do better work.

4.   I should learn to speak more carefully.

5.   You ought to walk faster, as it is getting late.

6.   I must be home before 9.

7.   It will be necessary for you to come back tomorrow.

8.   My friend's husband had to work late last night.

9.   You have to take your medicine now.

10. He has to get up early tomorrow morning.

11. We had to run to catch the bus.

12. It is necessary to get permission from the office before you can visit
     the classroom.

13. It isn't necessary to make an appointment.

14. He ought to be here before too long.

15. You should be ashamed of yourself!

16. I need some new clothes.

17. Will it be necessary for me to go to the doctor's office with you?

18. It wasn't necessary for you to wait for me.

19. That was an unnecessary expense. (Sign NOT for un-.)

20. Did you have to do that?

21. You must work harder or you'll fail the course.

22. Do you need any more help?

23. I don't need any help from you.

24. At what time should we meet you?

HOMEWORK ASSIGNMENT

"CLOZE" SENTENCES

Words for which signs will be taught in Lesson 6

1. Remember
2. Forget
3. Why
4. Most
5. Because
6. On
7. In
8. Out
9. With
10. Together
11. Going together
12. Far
13. Near
14. Around
15. Ask
16. Before
17. Better
18. Best

19. Big, large
20. Small, little
21. Keep
22. Borrow
23. Lend
24. Careful
25. Law
26. Rule
27. Mother-in-law
28. Father-in-law
29. Sister-(etc.) in-law
30. Aunt
31. Uncle
32. Cousin
33. Niece, nephew
34. Grandmother
35. Grandfather

1. Circle words for which you have been assigned to write sentences.

2. Write sentences on a separate sheet and turn in to your instructor at the beginning of the next class session.

NOTES

Signs taught in Lesson 5:

1.	Male	13.	Son	25.	Study
2.	Female	14.	Daughter	26.	Write
3.	Man	15.	Sister	27.	Pencil, pen
4.	Woman	16.	Brother	28.	Type, typewriter
5.	Child	17.	Marry, wed	29.	Secretary
6.	Baby	18.	Husband	30.	Lesson
7.	Boy	19.	Wife	31.	Paper
8.	Girl	20.	Which	32.	Print
9.	Gentlemen	21.	When (specific)	33.	Often
10.	Lady	22.	When (during)	34.	Sometimes
11.	Father	23.	Book	35.	Always
12.	Mother	24.	Read	36.	Never

Additional signs learned in class, or additional usages of above signs:

Other notes (including additional homework assigned by instructor, if any):

LESSON 6

1. REMEMBER: Sign KNOW or THINK, then with both hands in A-hand position, palms almost facing each other, press ball of right thumb to thumbnail of left thumb. (The first part of the sign can also be made with the thumb against the temple instead of fingertips.)

2. FORGET: Right hand in open-hand, fingers-closed position, palm to face and fingertips to left. Pass fingertips across forehead and off to one side an inch or two, closing hand to A-hand position, palm to self, as you do so.

3. WHY: Sign KNOW, then draw hand away and down, ending in Y-hand position, palm toward body.

4. MOST: Both hands in A-hand position, palms facing each other. Left hand remains stationary. Right hand moves up from below, brushing knuckles of left hand in passing and continues upward for a few inches.

5. BECAUSE: Sign KNOW, then quickly follow with MOST.

6. ON: Both hands in open-hand, fingers-closed position, palms to floor. Tap back of left hand with fingers of right hand.

7. IN: Both hands in and-hand position. Left hand palm to right, fingertips to right, knuckles to front. Place fingertips of right and-hand fingers and thumb.

8. OUT: Left hand in C-hand position and curled around right hand which is in open-and position, palm to floor, fingertips extending down below left hand. Draw right hand up through left hand above and to the right, BOTH hands closing to and-hands as the right hand passes through and out.

9. WITH: Both hands in A-hand position. Palms facing each other, knuckles forward. Bring them together from a few inches apart.

10. TOGETHER: Sign WITH, but after bringing hands together, move them forward a few inches.

11. GOING TOGETHER OR STEADY DATING: Sign TOGETHER two or more times.

12. FAR: Both hands in A-hand position, palms facing each other, hands
    touching. Left hand remains stationary, but right hand moves for-
    ward several inches toward right front.

13. NEAR: Both hands in right-angle hand-position, left hand near the body,
    right hand a few inches farther away. Bring right hand inward until
    the inside of the right hand's fingers rest on the backs of the left
    hand's fingers. (When object referred to is other than that repre-
    sented by the self, sign moves in the opposite direction.)

14. AROUND: Left hand in and-hand position, palm and fingertips toward
    ceiling. Right hand in index-hand position. Circle right index
    finger around fingertips of left hand.

15. ASK: (a) Both hands in open-hand, fingers-closed position. Bring palms
    together in a "praying" gesture, lowering them slightly after they
    are together.

       (b) (Slang version.) Left hand in index-hand position, fingertip
    toward ceiling and palm to right. Right hand in V-hand position,
    but with fingers crooked. Straddle left index finger between crooked
    V fingers of right hand.

       (c) Right index-hand. Crook index finger (making hand into an
    X-hand) pushing hand forward very slightly as you crook the finger.

16. BEFORE: Both hands in B-hand position. Left hand palm forward, finger-
    tips to ceiling. Right hand placed back to back with left hand (right
    palm toward body). Bring right hand back toward body a few inches.

17. BETTER: Right hand in open-hand, fingers-closed position, palm to body,
    fingertips to left. Pass fingertips across mouth, from left to right
    and close hand to A-hand position, palm to shoulder and thumb toward
    ceiling.

18. BEST: Sign GOOD, then MOST. Or sign BETTER, and when hand is in A-hand
    position, raise it several inches quickly until it is level with top
    of head.

19. BIG, LARGE: Both hands in L-hand position, palms to floor and fingertips
    to front. Start with hands close together but not touching, then
    separate hands widely.

20. SMALL, LITTLE: (a) Both hands in open-hand, fingers-closed position or
    slightly cupped palms facing each other, fingertips to front. Bring
    hands together without quite touching each other. Can be repeated
    once, separating hands an inch or two, then bring together again--
    still without touching.

       (b) With hand in "coin-flipping" position, move thumb upward in
    tiny strokes against ball of index finger.

       (c) Measure off a tiny space between thumb and index finger.

21. KEEP: Both hands in K-hand position, palms facing each other and finger-
    tips to front. Place right hand on top of left hand (little finger
    side of right hand against thumb side of left hand).

22. BORROW: Sign KEEP, but position hands farther away from body, then
    bring close to body.

23. LEND: Exactly the opposite of BORROW. Position hands close to body,
    then push out several inches. (Signed in the direction of the in-
    tended transfer.)

24. CAREFUL, BE CAREFUL: Sign KEEP, raising hands slightly after they are
    in KEEP position. (BE CAREFUL is frequently signed KEEP, KEEP.)

25. LAW: Left hand in open-hand, fingers-closed position, palm to right.
    Right hand in L-hand position. Place palm of right L on palm of
    left hand in a firm, definite gesture.

26. RULE: Similar to the sign for LAW except R-hand is used. Place right
    hand on palm of left hand twice, the R-hand moving slightly back
    toward wrist the second time.

27. MOTHER-IN-LAW: Sign MOTHER, then LAW (most common). Or MOTHER, IN, LAW.

28. FATHER-IN-LAW: Sign FATHER, then LAW. (Same comments apply as for
    MOTHER-IN-LAW.)

29. SISTER-IN-LAW, BROTHER-IN-LAW, SON-IN-LAW, DAUGHTER-IN-LAW: Same as
    above. Sign each--SISTER, BROTHER, SON, DAUGHTER--then follow the
    sign with the sign for LAW.

30. AUNT: Right hand in A-hand position, palm to front, knuckles to ceiling.
    Trace a short, vertical line from cheekbone to angle of jaw with
    thumb. Do this twice, rapidly.

31. UNCLE: Right hand in U-hand position, palm to front, fingertips to
    ceiling. Trace a line from hairline to temple with side of index
    finger. Do this twice rapidly.

32. COUSIN: Right hand in C-hand position, palm to left and fingertips to
    side of the face. Move fingertips back and forth from palm to body
    position to palm forward position. Repeat once.

33. NIECE, NEPHEW: Right hand in N-hand position, palm to front (or can
    face the cheek) knuckles to ceiling. For NIECE, circle N fingertips
    near cheek or jawbone. For NEPHEW, circle N fingertips near fore-
    head. (Small circles, please, or they will think you are signing
    CRAZY.)

34. <u>GRANDMOTHER</u>: Sign MOTHER, then when hand is open, describe a small
circle with right <u>open-hand, fingers-closed</u>; with left hand in <u>A-hand</u>
position, palm up, held waist high, opening to <u>5-hand</u> at the same
time the right hand opens.

35. <u>GRANDFATHER</u>: Sign like GRANDMOTHER, except that sign begins with FATHER
instead of MOTHER.

PRACTICE SENTENCES

<u>Note</u>: Write your recital sentences at the bottom of the list.

1. It would be better to ask around before you lend it to him.

2. Which girl is Jerry going with now?

3. Do you remember why we called this meeting?

4. Never a borrower or lender be if you wish friendship to grow warmer.

5. But if one or the other you must be, it is far better to be the former.

6. My aunt brought my cousins with her when she came.

7. Don't forget to bring your books.

8. She is mad at him because he forgot her birthday.

9. Be careful not to break the law.

10. My mother-in-law and father-in-law came to visit us on Sunday.

11.

12.

13.

14.

15.

HOMEWORK ASSIGNMENT

"CLOZE" SENTENCES

Words for which signs will be taught in Lesson 7

1. If
2. Somebody
3. Meet
4. Come, coming
5. Go, going
6. Away, gone
7. Through
8. River
9. Kiss
10. Every
11. Lassie
12. Laddie
13. Yet, still
14. All
15. Smile
16. At
17. From
18. Town, city, village

19. Greet
20. Frown, scowl, cross
21. Among
22. Crowd, group, class
23. There (poetic)
24. Sweetheart, boyfriend
25. Dear, dearly
26. Love
27. Where
28. Anywhere
29. Home
30. Choose, pick
31. Sing, song, music
32. Singer, musician
33. Pretty
34. Beautiful
35. Ugly

1. Circle the words for which you have been assigned to write sentences.

2. Write sentences on separate sheet and turn in to your instructor at the beginning of the next class session.

NOTES

Signs taught in Lesson 6:

1. Remember	13. Near	25. Law
2. Forget	14. Around	26. Rule
3. Why	15. Ask	27. Mother-in-law
4. Most	16. Before	28. Father-in-law
5. Because	17. Better	29. Sister- (etc.) in-law
6. On	18. Best	30. Aunt
7. In	19. Big, large	31. Uncle
8. Out	20. Small, little	32. Cousin
9. With	21. Keep	33. Niece, nephew
10. Together	22. Borrow	34. Grandmother
11. Going together	23. Lend	35. Grandfather
12. Far	24. Careful	

Additional signs learned in class, or additional usages of above signs:

Other notes (including additional homework assigned by instructor, if any):

LESSON 7

COMIN' THRU THE RYE

If a body meet a body
Comin' thru the Rye,
If a body kiss a body
Need a body cry?

Chorus:

Every Lassie has her laddie
Nane they say ha'e I,
Yet all the lads they smile at me
When comin' thru the Rye.

If a body meet a body
Comin' frae the town,
If a body greet a body
Need a body frown?

Chorus:

Every Lassie has her laddie
Nane they say ha'e I,
Yet all the lads they smile at me
When comin' thru the Rye.

Amang the train there is a swain
I dearly love mysel',
But what's his name or where's his hame
I dinna choose to tell.

Chorus:

Every Lassie has her laddie
Nane they say ha'e I,
Yet all the lads they smile at me
When comin' thru the Rye.

WORD-DESCRIPTIONS OF SIGNS

1. IF: Two <u>F-hands</u>, palms facing each other, fingertips pointing forward. Move up and down alternately.

2. SOMEBODY: Right <u>index-hand</u>, palm toward body, fingertip toward ceiling. Describe small circle with hand, using elbow as fulcrum (or pivot).

3. MEET: Both <u>index-hands</u>, fingers to ceiling and palms facing each other. Bring hands together until thumbs touch along their length. (Please note <u>index-hands</u>. Important!)

4. COME, COMING: (a) Both hands in <u>index-hand</u> position, palms toward body, fingers pointing to each other. Circle each index finger around the other, each circle bringing hands closer to body, circles moving counterclockwise in relation to right hand. (Platform version.)

   (b) (Conversational version.) Right <u>index-hand</u> makes a largish, beckoning gesture, ending sign with fingertip pointing to the floor in front of signer. (Both hands can be used in this sign, and, depending on the emphasis given it, the number of times it is repeated, can be used to indicate: a chronic dropper--a pest. Or a good friend who drops by frequently--or someone who keeps trying to catch you at home, <u>in vain</u>.)

   (c) Usually used as in invitation--or command. Same as COMING (b) except that <u>open-hand, fingers-closed</u> position is used.

5. GO, GOING: (a) (Not in poem, but handy to know at this point.) Exactly as COMING, but reverse direction of circles and move hands away from body. (Platform version.)

   (b) (Conversational version.) Right <u>index-hand</u> points to floor then moves away and up until finger is pointing to right front. (Same comments apply as in COMING (b) regarding use of both hands, emphasis or lack of it, and repetition of this sign.)

   (c) Same as in GOING (b) except that <u>right-angle</u> hand is used, and hand straightens out to <u>open-hand, fingers-closed</u> at the end of sign. (Most often used as a command: "Go away!")

6. AWAY, GONE (AWAY): Same as GOING (c).

7. THROUGH: Both hands in <u>open-hand, fingers-closed</u> position. Left hand faces body. Push outer edge of right hand through left hand, passing between second and third fingers of left hand.

8. <u>RIVER</u>: With both hands in <u>4-hand</u> position, palms down, put the right hand behind the left hand, then, wiggling the fingers, push both hands off to left-front to indicate rippling waves flowing down a river.

9. <u>RIVER (RYE)</u>: Generally spelled out, but for poems, it is signed like this: Make the letter R, then sign RIVER.

10. <u>KISS</u>: Right <u>open-hand, fingers-closed</u>, palm to body. Touch fingertips to mouth, then to cheek.

11. <u>EVERY</u>: Both <u>A-hands</u>. Left hand remains stationary. Palms facing each other. Brush knuckles of right hand downward twice against heel of left hand.

12. <u>LASSIE</u>: Sign FEMALE twice (GIRL).

13. <u>LADDIE</u>: Sign MALE twice (BOY).

14. <u>YET, STILL</u>: <u>Y-hands</u>, palms toward floor, both hands parallel and about six inches apart. Move hands forward in a down-and-up semicircle.

15. <u>ALL</u>: Both hands in <u>open-hand, fingers-closed</u> position. Left hand palm to self and fingertips to right. Right hand palm forward, fingertips to ceiling, alongside left hand. Pivot right hand at wrist and place <u>back</u> of right fingers against <u>palm</u> of left fingers. (This is the conversational version. In the platform version, the right hand exaggerates the pivoting movement to a large, sweeping circle.)

16. <u>SMILE</u>: Right <u>index-hand</u>. Trace an upward line from the corner of the mouth to describe a broad smile.

17. <u>AT</u>: Usually spelled out, but in <u>poetic</u> usage <u>only</u>, sign TO.

18. <u>FROM</u> (Used as "frae" in song): Left hand in <u>index-hand</u> position, palm to right, finger to ceiling. Right hand in <u>X-hand</u> position, palm to left. Put knuckle of right index (X) finger against knuckle of left index finger and pull right hand back a couple of inches. (Almost like pulling a bowstring back from a bow.)

19. <u>TOWN, VILLAGE, CITY</u>: Both hands <u>open-hand, fingers-closed</u> position. Palms almost facing each other. Touch fingertips to each other to make an inverted V, like a house roof. Move hands sideways, touching fingertips several times.

20. <u>GREET</u>: Sign HELLO. (Or pantomime lifting your hat and bowing.)

21. FROWN, SCOWL, CROSS: 5-hand, palm to face. Crook fingers to make a
    clawed-hand (and grimmace). Or push your nose up (head, too) with
    index fingertip, looking snooty. (This last for the song only.)

22. AMONG (Used as "amang" in song): Left hand in open-and hand-position,
    palm toward ceiling. Right hand in right-angle index-hand position,
    palm to floor. Circle right fingertip in and out and around left
    fingertips.

23. CROWD, GROUP, CLASS (Used for "twain" in song): Both slightly bent,
    curved 5-hands, fingers slightly spread, palms forward and separated
    by several inches. Move both hands outward in a circular movement,
    right hand circling to the right and left hand circling to the left,
    turning both hands so that palms face body and little fingers are
    almost, but not quite touching.

24. THERE: Right open-hand, fingers-closed position, palm to ceiling.
    Move slightly forward. (Or in a different poem, sweep it sideways
    from center front to right.)

25. SWEETHEART, BOYFRIEND (Used for "swain" in song): Sign MALE, then
    both hands in A-hand position, thumbs upward and palms to body.
    Bring hands together so knuckles are against knuckles--then wiggle
    thumbs up and down simultaneously.

26. DEARLY: Both hands, palms flat and facing body. Cross wrists and
    place palms against chest.

27. LOVE: Same as above, but use A-hands. (Actually DEAR and LOVE are
    interchangeable. But when they come together as in this poem, use
    one for LOVE and the other for DEARLY.)

28. HOME: Right and-hand. Bring fingertips to mouth to show putting
    something in the mouth, then open hand to open-hand, fingers-
    closed position and place palm on cheek to show BED. (Denotes
    bed and board.)

29. CHOOSE, PICK: F-hand, palm forward. Bring back several inches.

30. WHERE: (a) Right hand in index-hand position, palm forward and finger-
    tip to ceiling. Wiggle fingertip from side to side.

    (b) Sign like HERE, but make circles much larger. (Platform
    usage, generally, but also used in some localities to indicate
    conversational WHERE.)

31. PRETTY: Right hand in 5-hand position, palm to left and thumb point-
    ing to shoulder or ear. Move fingertips across the face (but not
    touching it) and downward in a circular motion, closing hand to
    and-hand position, palm to body, with hand to right of and along-
    side chin.

32. <u>BEAUTIFUL</u>: Sign PRETTY, then open hand quickly to <u>open-and</u> position, raising it a few inches as it opens.

33. <u>UGLY, HOMELY</u>: Right hand in <u>X-hand</u> position, palm to floor and knuckles to left. Place hand close to left side of nose and draw straight across the face without touching face. (This denotes the crooked nose some ugly people have.)

34. <u>SING, SONG, MUSIC</u>: Both hands in <u>open-hand, fingers-closed</u> position. Hold left arm out in a circle, palm facing self. Wave right hand back and forth (almost like a harp-playing gesture) in the circle of the left arm.

35. <u>SINGER, MUSICIAN</u>: Sign MUSIC, then -ER.

36. <u>ANY</u>: Right hand in <u>A-hand</u> position, palm to self, but slightly toward ceiling. Turn hand quickly to palm forward (but with palm facing slightly toward floor, too).

37. <u>ANYWHERE</u>: Sign ANY, and then WHERE. (A variation of this is ANY, WHAT, using the natural gesture WHAT, and using only the right hand.)

38. <u>ANYTHING</u>: Sign ANY, and then WHAT, WHAT, WHAT, using the one-handed natural gesture for WHAT, and moving the hand sideways between each WHAT.

PRACTICE SENTENCES

Note: Add your recital sentences to the bottom of the list.

1.   If you will stay a little longer, I will make some coffee.

2.   Somebody has to meet her when she arrives at the airport.

3.   They can't go with us tomorrow because Mary is sick.

4.   Joe was still there when everyone else had left.

5.   Kissing, while a lot of fun for the kissers, spreads colds.

6.   You all will have to study harder.

7.   I met Daphne in the city today.

8.   Bill scowled when I told him about the exam.

9.   Don't frown. It makes your pretty face look rather ugly.

10.   I couldn't find it anywhere even though I looked all around.

11.

12.

13.

14.

15.

HOMEWORK ASSIGNMENT

"CLOZE" SENTENCES

Words for which signs will be taught in Lesson 8

1. Neighbor
2. Friend
3. Enemy
4. Like
5. Dislike
6. Family
7. After
8. People
9. Things
10. Bring
11. Play
12. Make
13. Coffee
14. Clean, nice
15. Dirty
16. Find
17. Funny (amusing)
18. Funny (odd)

19. Fun
20. Make fun of
21. Here
22. Happy
23. Sad
24. See
25. Who
26. Look
27. Watch
28. Face, looks (like)
29. Want
30. Fly
31. Airplane
32. Ride (car)
33. Ride (horse)
34. Right (left)
35. Left (right)

1. Circle the words for which you have been assigned to write sentences.

2. Write sentences on separate sheet and turn it in to your instructor at the beginning of the next class session.

90

NOTES

Signs taught in Lesson 7:

1. If	13. Yet, still	25. Dear, dearly
2. Somebody	14. All	26. Love
3. Meet	15. Smile	27. Where
4. Come, coming	16. At	28. Anywhere
5. Go, going	17. From	29. Home
6. Away, gone	18. Town, city, village	30. Choose, pick
7. Through	19. Greet	31. Sing, song, music
8. River	20. Frown, scowl, cross	32. Singer, musician
9. Kiss	21. Among	33. Pretty
10. Every	22. Crowd, group, class	34. Beautiful
11. Lassie	23. There (poetic)	35. Ugly
12. Laddie	24. Sweetheart, boyfriend	

Additional signs learned in class, or additional usages of above signs:

Other notes (including additional homework assigned by instructor, if any):

LESSON 8

WORD-DESCRIPTIONS OF SIGNS

1. NEIGHBOR: Sign NEAR, then -ER.

2. FRIEND: Both hands in X-hand position. Place right index finger on top of left index finger and hook them together firmly. (You will quite often see this sign done twice, with fingers changing position until the left hand is on top of the right.)

3. ENEMY: Both hands in right-angle index position. Palms to body, fingertips touching each other. Separate hands quickly, then sign -ER.

4. LIKE (as opposed to dislike): Place thumb and second finger of right hand, fingers spread and palms to body, against chest. Move hand outward, closing fingers to an 8-hand position.

5. DISLIKE: Sign LIKE then turn hand to palm forward position vigorously, snapping it.

6. FAMILY: Both hands in F-hand position, palms facing forward. Put the tips of both index-thumb fingers together, then separate several inches, move them forward, simultaneously turning both hands to palm to body, then touch little finger edge of hands together, keeping both hands in F-hand position throughout sign.

7. AFTER: Both hands in B-hand position. Left hand palm to body, fingertips to right front. Right hand, palm to left. Touch little finger side of right hand to upper edge of left hand, then raise it and push it forward across the left hand a few inches. This also means ACROSS and OVER when that word is used to mean something like "over the river."

8. PEOPLE: Both hands in P-hand position (actually K-hands), palms and fingertips forward. Hold both hands up near the face or neck, and describe small, alternating circles forward and backward.

9. PLAY: Both hands in Y-hand position, palms facing body and thumbs to ceiling and little fingers to floor. Shake both hands up and down.

10. THING, THINGS: Right hand in open-hand, fingers-closed position, palm to ceiling. Lift and lower the hand an inch or two, moving it sideways each time you lift.

91

11. BRING: Both hands in <u>open-hand, fingers-closed</u> position, palms
    to ceiling. Place both hands to your right and several inches
    forward, then bring both hands back to a position directly in
    front of the body and close to it.

12. MAKE: Both hands in <u>S-hand</u> position. First part of sign, the
    right hand is placed on top of left hand, both palms facing
    body. Separate hands slightly, then second part of sign, the
    right hand is again placed on top of left, but the palms now
    face each other (or would, if hands were not one on top of the
    other). (Do NOT confuse this sign with COFFEE. Very common
    error.)

13. COFFEE: Both hands in <u>S-hand</u> position, palms to body. Left hand
    remains stationary. Right hand is placed on top of left, then
    moved in a coffee-grinding type circle.

14. CLEAN, NICE, PURE: Both hands in <u>open-hand, fingers-closed</u> position.
    Left palm faces ceiling, fingertips toward right front. Right
    palm faces floor, then slide it across left palm to left finger-
    tips. (Can use <u>P-hand</u> for PURE.)

15. DIRTY: Place back of right <u>5-hand</u>, fingertips to left front against
    underside of chin and wiggle fingers alternately.

16. FIND, FOUND: Almost like CHOOSE. Difference is in CHOOSE, the palm
    faces forward. In FOUND, you use an <u>F-hand</u>, palm to floor, fin-
    gertips forward. Bring hand back toward body, raising palm to
    palm forward position. Both the sign for CHOOSE and the sign for
    FIND end up the same way. The difference is in the beginning hand
    position.

17. FUNNY (Ha-Ha type): <u>H-hand</u>. Place fingertips on bridge of nose,
    then draw downward down nose, ending with hand in <u>N-hand</u> position,
    in front of face, repeating once, quickly.

18. FUNNY (PECULIAR), QUEER: Right hand in <u>C-hand</u> position, palm to left.
    Place hand in front of face (usually the nose), then rotate until
    palm is down toward floor. Hand remains in place, it just rotates.

19. FUN: Sign FUNNY, then, with both hands in <u>H-hand</u> position, palms
    to floor, strike the palms of right <u>H-hand</u> fingers across backs
    of left <u>H-hand</u> fingers.

20. MAKE FUN OF: Sign FUN, then bring <u>right H-hand</u> back up (striking
    left <u>H-hand</u> fingers as it comes up), then down again, <u>again</u> strik-
    ing left <u>H-hand</u> fingers as it passes downward.

21. HERE: Both hands, palms flat and facing ceiling. Describe small, flat horizontal circles with each hand, each hand moving in opposite directions.

22. HAPPY: Right hand open-hand, fingers-closed position. Place palm against chest and brush upward. Repeat once or twice.

23. SAD: Open hand, fingers spread slightly. Place in front of face and lower a few inches, with appropriately mournful expression on face.

24. SEE: Right hand in V-hand position. Palm toward body, fingertips to ceiling. Place fingertips on upper right cheek, then push forward a few inches.

25. LOOK: Sign SEE, but turn hand so fingertips point forward and palm is facing floor and move hand forward a few inches. (Used when you say something like, "Look at that gal's wacky hair-do.") This is NOT used to say, "It looks like rain," or "She looks like her Mother." These have their own signs which follow in this lesson.)

26. WATCH: Sign LOOK, but push the hand forward more vigorously, and place heel of right hand on back of left hand.

27. WHO: Right hand in right-angle index position, palm to self and fingertip pointing to chin. Move finger in little circles around chin.

28. FACE, LOOKS (LIKE): Similar to WHO, but fingertip circles whole face. This is used when you wish to say, "She looks like her mother." When you use it in this way, follow LOOKS with the sign for SAME or ALIKE.

29. WANT: Both hands in 5-hand position, palms to ceiling. (One hand can be used.) Crook fingers, while moving hand back toward self an inch or two.

30. FLY: Right hand in Y-hand or ILY position. Raise it over your head (palm to floor and knuckles facing forward), and push it forward several inches.

31. AIRPLANE: Sign FLY twice.

32. RIDE (in a car): Left hand in C-hand position, palm to right and thumb-index edge of hand on top. Sit fingers of right curved N-hand on thumb of left hand and move both hands forward a few inches.

94

33. RIDE (a horse): Left hand in open-hand, fingers-closed position,
palm to right, fingertips pointing forward. Right hand in V-hand
position, palm to floor and fingertips of V to floor. Straddle
edge of left palm with two fingers of the V-hand and gallop hands
forward in little hops.

34. RIGHT (opposite of left): Right hand in R-hand position. Move hand
to the right in a short, straight, abrupt movement.

35. LEFT: Like RIGHT above, except that L-hand is used, and the hand
moves to the left.

36. BELIEVE: Sign THINK, then MARRY.

PRACTICE SENTENCES

<u>Note</u>: Add your recital sentences to the bottom of the list.

1. Our neighbors have a beautiful house.

2. She has many friends because she has a nice personality.

3. Last year, Kevin and his family went to Europe.

4. People are funny sometimes.

5. It makes me happy to see the children having so much fun playing.

6. What happened to your new dress? It's all dirty.

7. It isn't always easy to make friends with children.

8. Do you like horseback riding?

9. After all our warnings, she still forgot to bring the can opener.

10. Who is watching the children?

11.

12.

13.

14.

15.

HOMEWORK ASSIGNMENT

"CLOZE" SENTENCES

Words for which signs will be taught in Lesson 9

1. Fast
2. Money
3. Buy
4. Shopping
5. Both
6. Quit
7. Late
8. Early
9. Finish
10. Grow, Spring
11. Summer
12. Autumn, Fall
13. Winter, cold
14. Any
15. Other
16. Anything
17. Eat, ate, food
18. Drink
19. Breakfast

20. Lunch
21. Dinner
22. Won't, refuse
23. Win
24. Lose (a game)
25. Lose (something)
26. Color
27. Red
28. Yellow
29. Blue
30. Green
31. Pruple
32. Black
33. Pink
34. White
35. Gray
36. Brown
37. Silver
38. Gold

1. Circle the words for which you have been assigned to write sentences.

2. Write sentences on separate sheet and turn it in to your instructor at the beginning of the next class session.

NOTES

Signs taught in Lesson 8:

1.	Neighbor	13.	Coffee	25.	Who
2.	Friend	14.	Clean, nice	26.	Look
3.	Enemy	15.	Dirty	27.	Watch
4.	Like	16.	Find	28.	Face, looks (like)
5.	Dislike	17.	Funny (amusing)	29.	Want
6.	Family	18.	Funny (odd)	30.	Fly
7.	After	19.	Fun	31.	Airplane
8.	People	20.	Make fun of	32.	Ride (car)
9.	Things	21.	Here	33.	Ride (horse)
10.	Bring	22.	Happy	34.	Right (left)
11.	Play	23.	Sad	35.	Left (right)
12.	Make	24.	See		

Additional signs learned in class, or additional usages of above signs:

Other notes (including additional homework assigned by instructor, if any):

LESSON 9

WORD-DESCRIPTIONS OF SIGNS

1. FAST: Both hands in L-hand position, palms facing each other, finger-tips to front, and one hand slightly closer to chest than the other. Crook index fingers as if pulling the trigger of a gun. Or right hand in T-hand position, palm to left, knuckles to front. Snap thumb up into air as if flipping a coin.

2. MONEY: Left hand in open-hand, fingers-closed position, palm facing ceiling. Right hand in and-hand position, palm to left. Pat backs of fingers against palm of left hand.

3. BUY: Sign MONEY, then bring right and-hand forward as if handing money to someone. (Palm facing ceiling.)

4. SHOPPING: Sign BUY, BUY rapidly.

5. BOTH: Left hand in C-hand position, palm to body, fingertips to right. Right hand in V-hand position, palm to body, fingertips to ceiling. Place backs of V-hand fingers against palm of left hand. Close left hand around the V-hand fingers and draw right hand down and out of left fist. (V-hand fingers closing to H-hand position as it passes through left hand.)

6. QUIT: Left hand in loose S-hand position, palm to right with knuckles forward. Right H-hand, palm to left. Close left hand around the two right H-hand fingers then draw fingers of right hand quickly up and out and back toward body.

7. LATE: Right open-hand, fingers-closed hand, palm to rear, fingertips to floor. Hold palm about waist level alongside the body. Wave fingertips forward and backward a couple of times. (Also used for HAVEN'T and NOT YET.)

8. EARLY: (a) (Gallaudet version.) Left hand in open-hand, fingers-closed position, palm to floor. Right hand in touch position. Touch tip of middle finger (other fingers remain extended) of right hand to back of left wrist, then bring heel of right hand against back of left wrist quickly, the right hand's fingers relaxing to a loose C-hand or sloppy A-hand configuration.

    (b) (Illinois version.) Touch tip of right index finger to nose (palm to self), then, with palm still facing self, lower hand quickly, ending with hand in Y-hand position (or NOW sign, made with one hand), palm to self.

9. FINISH: (a) FINISHED, ALREADY: 5-hand position, palm to body. Twist wrist quickly so palm faces forward.

   (b) END: Left hand in B-hand position, palm to body, finger-tips to right. Right hand in open-hand, fingers-closed position, palm to floor. Run palm of right hand along index finger edge of left hand to fingertips, then turn right hand to palm left and run palm across fingertips of left hand. (Denotes a "chopping off" of something.) Also means ALREADY HAVE or HAVE in some contexts. Often abbreviated to just the last, "chopping off" part of the sign when used as HAVE.

10. GROW, SPRING: Both hands in and-hand position. Left hand palm to right, fingertips to right. Push right hand through left hand from bottom (little finger side) upward, fingers of right hand opening as they come out at the top. (For SPRING, repeat this once, quickly.)

11. SUMMER: Right hand in X-hand position, palm to floor, knuckles to left. Draw across forehead from left to right (denotes wiping sweat off brow).

12. AUTUMN, FALL: Left hand and arm in NOON position. Right hand in B-hand position, palm to floor, fingertips to left. Bring index edge of right hand against elbow of left arm in two short, chopping "blows." (Denotes the slashing of trees in the fall for the maple sap.)

13. WINTER, COLD: Both hands in S-hand position, palms toward each other. Shake hands a couple of times to denote shivers from the cold.

14. OTHER: Exactly the reverse of ANY. Palm to floor, then to self.

15. EAT, ATE, FOOD: Right hand in and-hand position, palm to self. Bring fingertips to lips.

16. DRINK: Right hand in C-hand position, palm to left and knuckles pointing forward (as if holding a glass). Bring thumb to mouth and tilt hand as if tilting glass of water when drinking.

17. BREAKFAST: Sign EAT, then MORNING.

18. LUNCH: Sign EAT, then NOON.

19. DINNER: Sign EAT, then NIGHT.

20. WON'T, REFUSE: Right hand in A-hand position, palm to left and knuckles toward ceiling. Move hand backward abruptly until thumb bumps against shoulder. (Also means WOULDN'T.)

21. <u>WIN</u>: Sign GET, then raise hand as if to wave a flag with right hand--
    pretend you are holding a small pennant and whirling it.

22. <u>LOSE</u> (a game): Sign STAND (V fingertips of right hand "standing" on
    palm of left <u>open-hand, fingers-closed</u>), then "fall" (bring heel
    of right <u>V-hand</u> down to palm of left hand).

23. <u>LOSE</u> (something): Both hands in <u>right-angle hand</u> position, palms
    to self and fingertips to self. Touch backs of both sets of
    fingernails together, then move fingers downward, separating
    hands and opening fingers to spread position, fingertips to floor
    and palms facing each other.

24. <u>COLOR</u>: Right hand in <u>index-hand</u> position, palm to self and finger-
    tip pointing to ceiling. Touch fingertip to chin, then open
    hand to <u>5-hand</u> position and wave fingers in front of chin (wiggle
    them), palm to self.

25. <u>RED</u>: Right hand in <u>index-hand</u> position, palm to self and fingertip
    to ceiling. Draw fingertip down chin a couple of times. (De-
    rived from pointing to women's red lips.)

26. <u>YELLOW</u>: Right hand in <u>Y-hand</u> position. Turn hand from palm inward
    to palm outward several times, with a slight downward "dip" each
    time.

27. <u>BLUE</u>: Right hand in <u>B-hand</u> position. Turn hand palm inward then
    palm outward a couple of times, with fingertips "dipping" slightly
    each time.

28. <u>GREEN</u>: Right hand in <u>G-hand</u> position. Shake hand from palm inward
    to palm outward a couple of times.

29. <u>PURPLE</u>: Right hand in <u>P-hand</u> position. Follow above directions for
    shaking hand.

30. <u>BLACK</u>: Right hand in <u>right-angle index</u> hand, palm to left. Draw
    thumb edge of index finger across forehead.

31. <u>PINK</u>: Right hand in <u>P-hand</u> position, palm to self. Touch second
    finger of P to chin and draw downward an inch or so on the chin.

32. <u>WHITE</u>: Right hand in <u>5-hand</u> position. Place hand against center of
    chest, then draw it forward, closing hand to <u>and-hand</u> position a
    few inches in front of chest.

33. <u>BROWN</u>: Right hand in <u>B-hand</u> position, palm forward and fingertips
    to ceiling. Place thumb edge of index finger against cheekbone
    and draw whole hand downward to jaw line.

34. <u>GRAY</u>: Both hands in <u>5-hand</u> position, palms to self and fingertips pointing to each other. Brush fingertips of each hand back and forth against fingertips of other hand.

35. <u>SILVER</u>: Sign WHITE, then MONEY.

36. <u>GOLD</u>: Touch index finger of right hand to ear lobe, then sign YELLOW. (Denotes the gold of earrings.)

102

HOMEWORK ASSIGNMENT

"CLOZE" SENTENCES

Words for which signs will be taught in Lesson 10

1. Just (exactly)
2. Much (b)
3. Care (love)
4. Try
5. Hide
6. Ought
7. Haven't
8. So
9. Or
10. Heart
11. Prayer
12. Church
13. Temple
14. Some (indefinite)
15. Some (part of)
16. Way
17. Show (demonstrate)
18. Show (movie)
19. Show (play)

20. Swear (vow)
21. Let
22. Happen
23. Feel
24. Hate
25. Eager
26. Stubborn
27. Bother
28. Between
29. Interrupt
30. Silly
31. Misunderstand
32. Complain
33. Look for (seek)
34. Touch
35. Feel hurt
36. Feel depressed
37. Excite, thrill
38. Sensitive, sensitivity

1. Circle the words for which you have been assigned to write sentences.

2. Write sentences on separate sheet and turn it in to your instructor
    at the beginning of the next class session.

NOTES

Signs taught in Lesson 9:

1.	Fast	14.	Any	27.	Red
2.	Money	15.	Other	28.	Yellow
3.	Buy	16.	Anything	29.	Blue
4.	Shopping	17.	Eat, ate, food	30.	Green
5.	Both	18.	Drink	31.	Purple
6.	Quit	19.	Breakfast	32.	Black
7.	Late	20.	Lunch	33.	Pink
8.	Early	21.	Dinner	34.	White
9.	Finish	22.	Won't, refuse	35.	Gray
10.	Grow, Spring	23.	Win	36.	Brown
11.	Summer	24.	Lose (a game)	37.	Silver
12.	Autumn, Fall	25.	Lose (something)	38.	Gold
13.	Winter, cold	26.	Color		

Additional signs learned in class, or additional usages of above signs:

Other notes (including additional homework assigned by instructor, if any):

BREATHER SESSION NOTES

New signs learned:

Other notes:

LESSON 10

YOU'LL NEVER KNOW

You'll never know
Just how much I love you
You'll never know
Just how much I care

And if I tried
I still couldn't hide
My love for you

You ought to know
For haven't I told you so
A million or more times

You went away
And my heart went with you
I say your name
In my every prayer

If there is some other way
To prove that I love you
I swear I don't know how

You'll never know
If you don't know now.

WORD-DESCRIPTIONS OF SIGNS

1. JUST (exactly): Both hands in 20-hand position. Left hand palm to ceiling, knuckles forward. Right hand palm to floor, knuckles forward. Place fingertips of 20-fingers of right hand precisely on fingertips of left 20-hand.

2. MUCH: In poetic usage, this is signed like LARGE or BIG, with hands in cupped-hand position instead of L-hand position.

3. CARE: In poetic usage, this is signed like one variation of SELFISH, the description of which follows: Right hand in C-hand position, palm to self. Place fingertips on chin (knuckles to ceiling), then close hand to S-hand position, keeping hand close to chin.

4. TRY: Both hands in A-hand or T-hand position, palm to self, thumbs to ceiling. Move hands forward in a down and up movement, turning hands to palm forward position.

5. HIDE: Left hand in cupped-hand position, palm to floor, fingertips pointing to right front. Right hand in A-hand position, palm to left, knuckles pointing to left front. Touch right thumbnail to lips then move it forward and under left cupped hand, ending up with right hand "hidden" under left palm—or, in other words, left hand covering right hand, right thumb touching left palm.

6. OUGHT: Sign MUST, NECESSARY, and so on.

7. HAVEN'T: Sign LATE.

8. SO: Sign THAT (poetic license!).

9. OR: Left hand in L-hand position, palm facing body and index fingertip pointing to right front. Right hand in index-hand position, palm to floor. Touch right fingertip (index finger) to left thumb then to left index fingertip.

10. HEART: Both hands in index-hand position, palms to self. Touch both left and right fingertips to left chest and trace a heart, left fingertip tracing the left side of the heart and the right fingertip tracing the right side of the heart.

11. PRAYER: Natural sign. Place hands palm to palm in a praying gesture.

12. CHURCH: Left hand in open-hand, fingers-closed position, fingertips to right front and palm to floor. Right hand in C-hand position, palm forward. Place thumb joint against back of left palm. Repeat once.

13. TEMPLE: Same as CHURCH, but <u>T-hand</u> position instead of C-hand position is used.

14. SOME: In poetic usage, one should use the sign for SOMETHING or in other words, the same sign as "A body" in "Comin' thru the Rye."

15. SOME: (As in, "Some people just can't see dirt.") Both hands in <u>open-hand, fingers-closed</u> position. Left hand palm to body, fingertips to right front. Place heel edge of right hand (little finger edge), palm to left and fingertips pointing to left front, against left palm and draw it downward until edge of right little finger is in center of left palm.

16. WAY: Similar to LET, except that the forward motion of the hands is more pronounced and extends farther from the body.

17. SHOW (demonstrate): Left hand in <u>open-hand, fingers-closed</u> position, palm forward and fingertips to ceiling. Right hand in <u>index-hand</u> position, palm to self. Place right fingertip in center of left palm, then move both hands forward a few inches.

18. SHOW (movie): Both hands in <u>5-hand</u> position. Left hand palm to body, fingertips to right. Right hand palm facing left hand palm, fingertips to ceiling. Without touching hands, flicker the right hand back and forth across the left hand.

19. SHOW (play or drama): Both hands in <u>A-hand</u> position, palms forward and knuckles to ceiling. Raising both hands to shoulder level, move them alternately in and out in short, circular movements.

20. SWEAR (vow): Place right <u>index-hand</u> fingertip to mouth, then move right hand forward and to the right, opening it to <u>open-hand, fingers-closed</u> position, with palm facing outward and fingertips to ceiling--sort of like natural sign for HALT.

21. LET: Both hands in <u>open-hand, fingers-closed</u> position, palms facing each other and separated several inches. Push both hands forward several inches in a down and up motion (similar to WHEN (during) sign). You can also use <u>L-hands</u> for this sign.

22. HAPPEN: Both hands in <u>index-hand</u> position, palms to ceiling (or to each other), fingertips pointing forward. Rotate both hands to palm to the floor position, lowering them as you do so, and bringing them closer together. (You may encounter a situation wherein a deaf person, with a challenging expression on his face will say-- "What if. . . ." In other words, what if something should go wrong, or just in case. . . .)

23. FEEL: Right hand in <u>5-hand</u> position, with middle finger bent slightly toward palm. Place fingertip of middle finger against upper chest and draw upward a few inches.

24. FEEL HURT (emotionally): Sign FEEL, then flick hand outward (keep-
    ing hand in FEEL position, fingerwise) as if shaking a drop of
    water off your middle finger.

25. DEPRESSED, DISCOURAGED: Sign FEEL, but after hand has risen upward
    on chest, run it lightly back downward nearly to the waistline.

26. EXCITED: With both hands, sign FEEL, but bring both hands upward
    and off the chest completely. A variation of this is to have
    the hands alternate while doing this. This usually means EXCITING.
    Can also be used to mean THRILL.

27. TOUCH: Right hand in FEEL position, but instead of touching chest,
    middle finger touches back of left palm.

28. HATE: Both hands in 8-hand position, palms forward, fingertips to
    ceiling. Open hands to 5-hand position quickly, moving them for-
    ward abruptly.

29. EAGER, ZEALOUS: Both hands in open-hand, fingers-closed position,
    fingertips forward. Place palms together and rub them back and
    forth.

30. STUBBORN: Right hand in B-hand position, palm forward and finger-
    tips to ceiling. Place thumb-edge of hand against forehead, and
    keeping it there, bend hand to right-angle hand-position. Or you
    can place your thumb against your temple while doing this.

31. BETWEEN: Left hand in open-hand, fingers-closed position with thumb
    extended, palm to right self, fingertips pointing to right front.
    Right hand in B-hand position, palm to left and fingertips to
    left front. Place little finger edge of right hand between thumb
    and index finger of left hand and rock hand (right hand) back and
    forth from left to right and back again.

32. BOTHER: Hands in same position as for BETWEEN, but instead of rock-
    ing right hand back and forth, hit left palm against membrane
    between thumb and index finger of left palm with little finger
    edge of right hand a couple of times.

33. INTERRUPT: Hands in same position as for above, but hit little finger
    edge of right hand ONCE against base of left thumb (on membrane
    of thumb of left hand).

34. SILLY: Right hand in Y-hand position, palm to self. Brush thumb
    several times against side of nose. Also means FOOLISH.

35. MISUNDERSTAND: Right hand in V-hand position, palm to self and finger-
    tips to ceiling. Touch fingertips of V to forehead (balls of the
    fingertips), then turn hand to palm outward and touch fingernails
    of V to the same place on the forehead.

36. <u>COMPLAIN</u>: Right hand in <u>clawed-hand</u> position, palm to self. Touch fingertips to chest (thumb, too) a couple of times.

37. <u>SEEK, LOOK FOR</u>: Right hand in <u>C-hand</u> position, palm to left. Describe circle in front of eyes. (Denotes the looking for something through a telescope.)

38. <u>SENSITIVE, SENSITIVITY</u>: (a) Touch middle fingertip of right <u>touch-hand</u> to left chest (above heart) twice.

    (b) Touch middle fingertip of right <u>touch-hand</u> to back of left hand (actually, sign TOUCH twice).

110

HOMEWORK ASSIGNMENT

"CLOZE" SENTENCES

Words for which signs will be taught in Lesson 11

1. First, second, etc.
2. Tenth, eleventh, etc.
3. Last
4. Finally
5. Young
6. New
7. Next
8. Give (formal)
9. Give (slang)
10. Full
11. Enough
12. Empty, naked, bare
13. Hot
14. Bald

15. Mind going blank
16. Warm
17. Cool
18. Hold
19. Hurt
20. Enter (into)
21. Kind (kindly)
22. Kind (type)
23. Mean (unkind)
24. Mean (intend)
25. Laugh
26. Hard, difficult
27. Sunny (personality)

1. Circle the words for which you have been assigned to write sentences.

2. Write sentences on separate sheet and turn it in to your instructor at the beginning of the next class session.

NOTES

Signs taught in Lesson 10:

1. Just (exactly)	14. Some (indefinite)	26. Stubborn
2. Much (b)	15. Some (part of)	27. Bother
3. Care (love)	16. Way	28. Between
4. Try	17. Show (demonstrate)	29. Interrupt
5. Hide	18. Show (movie)	30. Silly
6. Ought	19. Show (play)	31. Misunderstand
7. Haven't	20. Swear (vow)	32. Complain
8. So	21. Let	33. Look for (seek)
9. Or	22. Happen	34. Touch
10. Heart	23. Feel	35. Feel hurt
11. Prayer	24. Hate	36. Feel depressed
12. Church	25. Eager	37. Excite, thrill
13. Temple		

Additional signs learned in class, or additional usages of above signs:

Other notes (including additional homework assigned by instructor, if any):

PART II: INTERMEDIATE SECTION:
THE IDIOMATIC LANGUAGE OF SIGNS

INTERMEDIATE SECTION

At this point, the student who has successfully mastered the material in the first section of this manual may begin to consider himself no longer a beginner in manual communication, but an intermediate student. From this point onward, increasing emphasis in the course will be placed upon the idio-matic language of signs, rather than the language of signs as a pictographi-cal representation of the English language. This, in essence, means that the student will begin to learn to use the language of signs the way deaf people themselves use it, with all the grammatical idiosyncracies, dialectical peculi-arities, and idiomatic expressions which make the language of signs unique and picturesque.

Because the student who has reached the intermediate stage of his learning is assumed to have developed considerable facility at remembering signs with less repetition and reinforcement than was necessary during the beginning stage of his learning, fewer word-descriptions are provided in this section than was the case in the beginning section. This does not mean that there will be fewer new signs to learn. Quite the contrary, in fact, for the student will be in-creasing his vocabulary of signs at a far faster rate than ever before. The difference lies in that the student will be given a tremendous number of "extra" signs to learn, signs which will be taught as the need arises in the course of learning how to paraphrase, define, and transliterate idioms in English into the idiomatic language of signs and the reverse. Since the classroom dynamics will be such that the instructor will increasingly be permitting classroom dis-cussions to dictate much of the material for which he will teach the signs, it is not possible to furnish word-descriptions for every sign which could con-ceivably be learned as a result of such discussions. Therefore, only a bare framework of signs is provided in each lesson hencetoforth in the way of word-descriptions upon which the instructor and the students can build a much larger vocabulary of signs during any given lesson. This means that the burden of re-membering the extra signs is placed upon the student's own shoulders, for he will not have the "crutch" of the word-descriptions to rely upon in the event he forgets a sign. He should, therefore, make every effort to immediately use the new, extra signs a sufficient number of times so that they will become a part of his repertoire and not be forgotten.

From this point onward, also, practice sentences are not provided, but a blank page has been provided upon which the student can compose his own, as well as use for notes about signs learned in class and ways in which they are used.

Note: The student will find extremely helpful the booklet by Madsen (Bibli-ography) which expands on many of the concepts outlined in this section. It is recommended that this booklet be purchased and used as a supplementary textbook along with the present workbook.

LESSON 11

EXCERPTS FROM: CONCEPT ANALYSIS OF THE
IDIOMATIC LANGUAGE OF SIGNS[1]

A student who has completed one or two semesters of training in the language of signs and fingerspelling and sets out to put his newly acquired skills to use in conversing with deaf people, often finds himself in the position of a foreigner with a limited command of English attempting to follow rapid, dialectical and idiomatic English as spoken by the native American. It is understandable that such a student often feels lost, and begins to doubt his own ability as well as the comprehensiveness of the material his instructor used to train him. One factor often overlooked by the student in his confusion is that it is not usually his vocabulary of signs which is at fault, for when one stops to consider, one will usually recognize that many or most of the signs used by deaf people are understood by the student by the time he has had at least two semesters of training. It is the way in which the signs are put together--the way they are used--which baffles the student and prevents his comprehension of what is being said. Just as the English language has its idioms and local dialectical variations which baffle and confuse a foreigner trying to apply classroom-acquired knowledge of formal English to the rapid conversational exchange of words among ordinary Americans, the language of signs also has its idioms, figures of "speech," local dialects, subtleties of mood and implication, and its "rules." Until the student has mastered this idiomatic sign language, he cannot claim to have mastered the art of communicating with deaf people, however adept he may become at the formal language of signs as a pictographical approximation of English. Nor will he be able to fully appreciate the amazing versatility of the language of signs, in which a wide range of emotions, meaning, and information can be conveyed by a few signed and fingerspelled words--which may or may not bear any resemblance to the English language in grammatical structure or syntax.

Complicating the student's attempts to make himself understood in the language of signs is the well-recognized fact that the majority of deaf people today have had little exposure to, and therefore scant understanding of, the idioms of the English language itself. When the student signs and fingerspells in the formal language of signs a common idiom such as "he is a deadbeat," the deaf person to whom this is said may either not understand at all--or misinterpret the statement to mean "he was beaten dead" or "he should be beaten to death"--or, if he is slightly more sophisticated, "he is dead beat (tired)." Only the highly verbal, well-educated deaf person would understand that the student was telling him that a certain man was a chronic nonpayer of his debts.

---

[1] Babbini, Barbara E. Unpublished workbook for intermediate advanced students. Institute for Research on Exceptional Children, University of Illinois, Urbana, Illinois, 1970.

By the same token, a deaf person might say to the student in the course of a conversation "Think self." The unwary student might assume that this inexplicable combination of signs meant that he was being asked to think of himself, or asked what he thought, or that the deaf person was saying that he considered the student to be at fault for something, and so on. Only the student who has become aware of the idiosyncracies of the idiomatic language of signs would (if he had not encountered that particular expression before) be able to figure out that he was being told to use his own judgment, to suit himself, to make up his own mind, or to draw his own conclusions about something.

Another facet of the language of signs is that one sign can be used for many different words depending upon the context of what is being said. If the concept in a word for which no sign exists is similar in meaning to one for which a sign exists, that sign is often used for the word without a sign. Examples of this are the words OUGHT TO, HAVE TO, SHOULD, NECESSARY, MUST-- all of which have the common denominator of implied need, need to act, or need to conform to certain standards, and all of which are indicated by the single sign for NEED. On the other hand, there are also words for which the signs change according to the concept being expressed. One does not use the same sign for TRAIN when one speaks of a railroad train, for example, that one would use when speaking of training one's dog.

Along with the conceptual factors there are changes or differences in meaning lent by emphasis or lack of it, by nodding or shaking of the head, by the facial expression assumed by the speaker. For instance, the words "You will" can, depending upon the emphasis placed upon the signs, change from the question "You will?" to "YOU will?" or from a simple confirmation-seeking question to scathing sarcasm. Or, it can change from "You will (pass that exam, I'm sure)" to "You WILL (or I'll spank the pants offa you)"--all by varying the facial expression and the amount of emphasis placed upon the individual words separately or as a unit. Or, the positive statement "You understand" can be changed to the negative "You (don't) understand" by the speaker's shaking his head--or to a question by raising the eyebrows with a questioning look.

There are several words, also, which are used by themselves to transmit a complete sentence--the meaning of which changes subtly according to the facial expression and amount of emphasis used. To exemplify this, the word FOR can be used to indicate "What for?" or "Oh heck, what do I have to do that for?," or "Why in the name of Heaven did you do that?" If one notes that "idea," "why," "yes," and "no" can also be varied in this way when used as single sign responses, one begins to appreciate the importance of emphasis and facial expression to the meaning of what is being said.

Directionality--or the direction in which the sign is made--is also important to meaning. A single sign response such as "no," made with the fingertips pointing toward one, means that the speaker himself has been or will be refused something, whereas if it is made with the fingertips pointing toward the listener, it means the listener has been or will be refused something. And, furthermore, when the fingertips point neither at the speaker nor the listener, but in some generalized direction away from the speaker, it means that somebody has or is going to say "no" to something.

Since most students in classes in the language of signs are those with normal hearing, of interest also are homonymns (words that sound alike, but are spelled different) and homorphemes (words that look alike, but sound different). For the student who aspires to become an interpreter for deaf people, these words can be a trap into which he, in common with even veteran interpreters, can oftimes fall. TO, TWO, and TOO all sound alike--but are signed quite differently, as are THERE, THEIR, and THEY'RE. Also commonly missigned are HER (possessive pronoun, as in "her coat") and HER (object, as in "I told her"), which both sound alike and are spelled alike, but which have different signs which are often confused.

Finally, there is the growing emphasis on "new" signs, some of which have rapidly been accepted and put into use by both the deaf people themselves and those who work or associate with them. Among those granted almost immediate acceptance and utilized are the first-letter signs in which the first letter of the word being signed is incorporated into the "old" sign. Examples of this are TRY, RESPONSIBILITY, PLACE, LIVE, FAMILY, FREE, MEAN (in the sense of meaning), USE, SITUATION--all of which have "old" signs to which the first letter of each of the words has been added. Other "new" signs have been less successful in gaining acceptance, probably because of limited possibilities of their being used in daily conversation among deaf people not involved in educational programs, or, in some cases, because the "new" sign bears little resemblance to an "old" sign it is designed to replace or supplant, and because the "new" sign cannot be used with as much versatility as the "old" one could. A few of the "new" signs have partially succeeded in replacing "old" signs, however, particularly in the conjugations of the verb TO BE. The "old" language of signs had but one sign for all of the conjugations--AM, ARE, IS, BE, and so on, were all denoted by the same index-finger sign--whereas the "new" language of signs provides different alphabet letters for each in combination with the "old" sign movement and direction. The student, therefore, may find himself encountering both "old" and "new" signs as well as variations in idiom, dialect, facial expressions, emphasis--and individual idiosyncracies in style of performing any given sign, as well as in fingerspelling.

The examples which follow are designed to give the student in manual communication a start toward learning the patterns of grammatical structure in the language of signs, particularly those which differ from the structure of the English language. The examples given are by no means exhaustive, nor are the suggested substitute ways of signing the example sentences the only ways to express the concepts in the example sentences. In every case, attempts were made to provide the most common method of translating the concept in the sentence, but there will be regional variations as well as additional ways of transmitting the concept in idiomatic sign language which are precluded by space limitations. The instructor in a class in manual communication or interpreting for deaf people can probably give examples of further ways to paraphrase or interpret the example sentences in this manual.

118

It is hoped, however, that the students and the instructor will use this material primarily to build upon, to increase their awareness of the complexities of the idiomatic language of signs, and to further the development of their ability to identify and interpret other idiosyncracies not illustrated herein.

<u>Note</u>: A limited number of copies of the full booklet on Concept Analysis of the Idiomatic Language of Signs is available upon request from the author. However, the Madsen booklet previously mentioned is recommended.

EXAMPLES OF TRANSLATIONS OF COMMONLY USED SENTENCES
INTO IDIOMATIC SIGN LANGUAGE

In the examples below, the multiple conceptual meanings of a given word are illustrated in sentences commonly used by people with normal hearing. Immediately beneath each sentence is given the "translation" into idiomatic sign language of the concept of the word as implicit in the context of the sample sentence. In other words, what the word _means_ in the sentence context is translated into idiomatic sign language best understood by the majority of deaf people today. Students should take notes on other ways of translating the given sample sentences into idiomatic sign language which their instructor may be able to show them.

ABOUT

1. I was <u>just about</u> ready to give up.

    almost

2. He <u>abruptly faced about</u> and marched off.

    pantomime turning abruptly, using two <u>index hands</u>

3. He lives <u>about</u> a mile from me.

    about

4. I lost my earring somewhere <u>about</u> here.

    around or area

5. She is finally up and <u>about</u> again after that long illness.

    around or associating

Others:

LIGHT

1. Will you <u>light</u> the fire for me, please?

       pantomime striking a match and putting it to something
       or "start"

2. <u>Turn out the lights</u>, please.

       pantomime lights going off

3. She was wearing a coat that was too <u>light</u> and almost froze.

       light-<u>weight</u> sign

4. She <u>made light of</u> the situation.

       fun, or "think easy"

5. She had on a <u>light</u> blue dress.

       use sign for light (as opposed to dark)

6. There isn't enough <u>light</u> in here.

       brightness

7. I ate a <u>light</u> lunch.

       light-weight

8. I slept very <u>lightly</u> last night.

       light-weight

9. The medicine made me very <u>light-headed</u>.

       dizzy

10. The birds <u>light on</u> trees.

       pantomime birds perching on twigs

11. Teacher seems to feel <u>light-hearted</u> tonight.

       happy or light-weight feel (touching heart)

12. <u>The light finally dawned upon me.</u> (idiom)

       rephrase to: "It finally think appear to me." (FINALLY
       is signed like LAST)

13. Homer really was <u>lit</u> at the party last night.

        drunk

14. The house was all <u>lit up</u> when we got home.

        pantomime, with both hands, many overhead lights going on

    <u>Note</u>: There are many more ways to sign LIGHT, all having to do with direction in which the light shines--that is, in the face, headlights of a car shining forward, a flashlight wavering around, sunlight, spotlights, and so on, all or most of which are signed with the same basic "light going on" sign in which the hands begin the sign in <u>and-hand</u> position and open to <u>open-and</u> hand-position. The direction, position, and use of one or two hands will determine what kind of light is being talked about, as well as which of the many LIGHT signs you should use. In addition, there are the GLOW signs to further describe kinds of light--sunrise light, sunset light, firelight, twinkling lights of a city or town in the distance, and so forth.

Others:

LIKE

1. I <u>like</u> pie, especially cherry pie.

        like (opposite of dislike)

2. It <u>looks like</u> rain.

        seems going to

3. You <u>look like</u> your mother.

        face same

4. That is a <u>likely</u> story.

        Put an "Oh sure" expression on your face then say
        "That is a true ? story."

122

5. If you _like_ ----.

   like want

6. He is _like_ his father in that.

   same (using _Y-hand_ sign for SAME)

Others:

APPEAR

1. She _appears_ to be a nice person.

   seems

2. He _appeared before_ the judge to answer the charges.

   confronted, faced

3. A hole _appeared in the face_ of the dam.

   appeared in front

4. _Apparently_ he was mistaken about that.

   seems

Others:

9. <u>FULL</u>: Left hand in S-hand position, palm to the right and knuckles
   facing forward. Right hand in <u>open-hand, fingers-closed</u> position,
   palm to floor and fingertips to left-front. Draw right palm across
   left fist (top edge) from right to left.

10. <u>ENOUGH</u>: Exactly as in FULL, except that palm of right hand is drawn
    across top of left fist from <u>left</u> to <u>right</u> twice.

11. <u>EMPTY</u>: Left hand in <u>open-hand, fingers-closed</u> position, palm to floor
    and fingertips to right front. Right hand in <u>5-hand</u> position with
    middle finger bent slightly toward palm. Right hand palm to floor,
    fingertips pointing to left-front. Draw middle fingertip of right
    hand across back of left hand from wrist to knuckles.

12. <u>BALD</u>: Like EMPTY, except middle finger of right hand traces a path
    from center of forehead to center of back of head.

13. <u>MIND GOING BLANK</u>: Like BALD, above, except that middle finger traces
    a line <u>across forehead</u> above eyebrows from temple to temple.

14. <u>HOT</u>: Right hand in <u>C-hand</u> position, palm to body. Place fingertips
    against chin, then snap hand to palm outward (or to floor) position
    quickly, as if one had burned one's fingers.

15. <u>COOL, PLEASANT</u>: Both hands in <u>open-hand, fingers-closed</u> position, palms
    toward self and hands positioned on either side of face/jaw (about
    twelve inches apart). Bending hands at <u>palm</u>, move fingertips up
    and down in a "fanning" motion (as if fanning yourself with your
    fingertips).

16. <u>SUNNY (personality)</u>: Like COOL, above, except that fingers are rippled
    alternately instead of moving up and down as a unit.

17. <u>HOLD</u>: Both hands in <u>C-hand</u> position, palms to floor and knuckles facing
    forward. Close both hands to <u>S-hand</u> position, bringing them back a
    few inches toward body. (This sign depends upon what you are holding.
    Pantomime is important here. A rope? A child's hand, a boat--or what?)

18. <u>HURT</u>: Both hands in <u>right-angle index</u> hand-position, palms facing each
    other, knuckles facing front, hands separated by several inches. Bring
    index fingertips a few inches closer to each other in a sharp, abrupt
    motion.

19. <u>ENTER, INTO</u>: Left hand in <u>open-hand, fingers-closed</u> position, right hand
    in <u>B-hand</u> position. Both hands palm to floor. Left hand fingertips
    pointing to right-front, right hand fingertips forward. Left hand
    remains stationary. Place back of right hand fingers against palm of
    left hand index-finger edge, then move right hand forward and under
    left palm, keeping back of right hand against left palm. (Not <u>really</u>
    as complicated as it sounds.)

20. <u>KIND (kindly)</u>: Place right index finger (palm to left) against chin, then follow with the following: both hands in <u>right-angle</u> hand-position, palms facing each other, knuckles forward. Circle finger-tips of each hand around fingertips of other hand in a clockwise motion.

21. <u>KIND (as in "What kind of ----?")</u>: Fingerspell!

22. <u>MEAN (unkind)</u>: Place right <u>cupped-hand</u> fingertips, palm to body, against chin then close both hands to <u>A-hand</u> position, palms to each other and thumbs on top. Brush knuckles or right hand downward against left hand ONCE. (Second part of this sign is much like EACH or EVERY, but knuckles are brushed downward just once instead of twice.)

23. <u>MEAN (intend)</u>: Left hand palm upward, <u>open-hand, fingers-closed</u> position, fingertips pointing to right front. Right hand in <u>M-hand</u> position with fingers extended. Place fingertips of right hand against palm of left hand, raise them, rotate hand slightly, then place fingertips against palm of left hand again.

24. <u>LAUGH</u>: Like SMILE, only you repeat it once or twice swiftly. There are many variations of this.

25. <u>HARD (difficult)</u>: Both hands in <u>V-hand</u> position, but with fingers crooked. Left hand palm downward, knuckles to right-front. Right hand palm to ceiling, knuckles to left-front. Bring right hand down vigorously on top of left hand, knuckles meeting back to back. Can also be signed with both hands in <u>S-hand</u> position, but the "crooked 'V'" is more common.

26. <u>WARM</u>: Right hand in <u>C-hand</u> position, palm to self. Place backs of fingertips against underside of chin, then straighten hand in an upward and outward motion, ending with <u>open-hand, fingers-closed</u> position a few inches in front of the mouth.

Words for which signs will be taught in Lesson 12[1]

1.	Light	11.	Close
2.	Dark	12.	Under
3.	Live	13.	Over
4.	Address	14.	Put
5.	Long	15.	Pull
6.	Short	16.	Run
7.	Maybe	17.	Walk
8.	Only	18.	Stand
9.	Use	19.	Sit
10.	Open	20.	Fall (down)

[1]Many of the words above are signed several different ways, depending upon the meaning of the word in context of the sentence. For this reason, it will be unnecessary to construct Cloze sentences for these particular words. You will find many such sentences in the examples given in the concept analysis booklet you will receive along with this list.

NOTES

Signs taught in Lesson 11:

1. First, second, etc.	12. Empty, naked, bare	21. Kind (kindly)
2. Tenth, eleventh, etc.	13. Hot	22. Kind (type)
3. Last	14. Bald	23. Mean (unkind)
4. Finally	15. Mind going blank	24. Mean (intend)
5. Young	16. Warm	25. Laugh
6. New	17. Cool	26. Hard, difficult
7. Next	18. Hold	27. Sunny (personality)
8. Give (formal)	19. Hurt	
9. Give (slang)	20. Enter (into)	
10. Full		
11. Enough		

Additional signs learned in class, or additional usages of above signs:

Other notes (including additional homework assigned by instructor if any):

LESSON 12

WORD-DESCRIPTIONS OF SIGNS

1. LIGHT (as opposed to dark): Both hands in and-hand position, palms facing each other, fingertips facing each other and touching. Move hands upward and outward, separating them and opening them to 5-hand position, palms facing body.

2. DARK: Both hands in open-hand, fingers-closed position, palms to body. Hold hands out in front of yourself, at about face level, fingertips to ceiling. Cross hands in front of chest, fingertips of left hand facing right and right hand facing left, palms remaining toward body.

3. LIVE (I live in Podunkville): Can use either one or both hands. Hands can be in either L-hand or A-hand position. Palm to body, thumb toward ceiling. Place hand (or hands) on chest, then brush upward a few inches.

4. ADDRESS: Sign HOME, then LIVE, using A-hand position.

5. LONG: Left hand in open-hand, fingers-closed or B-hand position. Palm to floor. Draw right index finger along back of left hand and up the arm as far as you care to go. Distance you draw the finger denotes length--the shorter, the shorter, and so on.

6. SHORT: Both hands in H-hand position--or rather, sign NAME, then move the right H back and forth along the left H. (Note to teacher: Be sure students do not confuse this with CUT.)

7. MAYBE: Both hands in open-hand, fingers-closed position, palms to ceiling and fingertips forward. Move hands up and down in a "balancing" motion. (Also used to indicate MIGHT as in "I might do that.")

8. ONLY: Sign SOMEBODY.

9. USE: Right hand in U-hand position, fingertips to ceiling and palm forward. Move hand in a circular motion, keeping fingertips and palms facing the same way as described. Also used to mean WEAR, as in "I will wear my red dress."

10. OPEN: Both hands in B-hand position, palms forward and fingertips to ceiling. Place index-edges of both hands together, then separate them, rotating hands, palms facing each other position and separated by a few inches. Denotes double doors opening.

137

11. CLOSE: Reverse of OPEN. Have hands in palm facing each other position, then close them to palms forward, index-edge of hands touching each other.

12. UNDER: Left hand in open-hand, fingers-closed position, palm to floor and fingertips to right front. Right hand in A-hand position, palm to left and thumb on top. (Thumb extended, please.) Move right hand under left palm but not touching it.

13. OVER: Both hands in open-hand, fingers-closed position, palms to floor, fingertips facing (left to right-front and right to left-front) forwardish. Move right palm above left hand, moving from right to left. Do not touch left hand with right.

14. PUT: Both hands in and-hand position, palms and fingertips forward. Move both hands forward a few inches--or if you are asking someone to put something on a table, say, push the hands toward the table.

15. PULL: Natural sign. Pretend to grab a rope and pull.

16. RUN: Both hands in L-hand position, palms to floor and index fingers pointing forward, touch thumbs together, then crook index fingers a couple of times. In this case, the index fingers denote the legs. (This is used ONLY for the action verb as in "running to catch a bus." There are forty-seven different ways to sign RUN.)

17. WALK: Both hands in B-hand position, palms to floor and fingertips forward. Since the hands in this sign denote the feet, walk them forward, moving fingertips from forward position to fingertips-to-floor and back alternately.

18. STAND: Left hand in open-hand, fingers-closed position, palm to ceiling and fingertips forward. Stand the fingertips of right V-hand on palm of left hand.

19. SIT: Both hands in H-hand position, with fingers crooked. Both palms to floor, fingertips of H's facing floor also. Sit the right H on left H.

20. FALL (down): Sign STAND, then rotate right hand quickly to palm upward position, bumping back of right hand against left palm. (Many variations of this though.)

HOMEWORK ASSIGNMENT

"CLOZE" SENTENCES

Words for which signs will be taught in Lesson 13

1. Start
2. Keys
3. Stop
4. Take
5. Wash
6. Sick
7. Well
8. Weak
9. Feebleminded
10. Strong
11. Powerful

12. Anyway, doesn't matter
13. Wish, hunger, hungry
14. Desire, yearn
15. Thirsty
16. Vegetables
17. Potatoes
18. Onions
19. Tomatoes
20. Pumpkin
21. Water
22. Watermelon

1. Circle the words for which you have been assigned to write sentences.

2. Write sentences on separate sheet and turn in to your instructor at the beginning of the next class session.

NOTES

Signs taught in Lesson 12:

1. Light	9. Use	15. Pull
2. Dark	10. Open	16. Run
3. Live	11. Close	17. Walk
4. Address	12. Under	18. Stand
5. Long	13. Over	19. Sit
6. Short	14. Put	20. Fall (down)
7. Maybe		
8. Only		

Additional signs learned in class, or additional usages of above signs:

Other notes (including additional homework assigned by instructor if any):

LESSON 13

WORD-DESCRIPTIONS OF SIGNS

1. <u>START</u>: Left hand in <u>open-hand, fingers-closed</u> position, palm to right and fingertips half-way between forward and toward ceiling. Right hand in <u>index-hand</u> position, palm to floor. Place tip of right index finger between first and second fingers on left hand, then turn right hand to palm to self position, finger remaining between fingers of left hand. Denotes the turning of an ignition key.

2. <u>KEYS</u>: Signed like START, but uses <u>X-hand</u> position and does not go between fingers of left hand.

3. <u>STOP</u>: Both hands in <u>open-hand, fingers-closed</u> position. Left hand palm to ceiling, fingertips to right front. Right hand, palm to left, fingertips forward. Bring right hand sharply down until the little finger edge of right hand hits the center of left palm.

4. <u>TAKE</u>: Put out hand, palm to floor, grasp an imaginary something and bring it close to body.

5. <u>WASH</u>: Natural signs. If you are washing your face, make a face washing gesture. If washing hands, ditto. If washing clothes, pretend you are using an old washboard. If washing a car, pretend you are washing the roof of the car, and so forth.

6. <u>SICK</u>: Right hand in <u>5-hand</u> position. Bend middle finger down toward palm. Touch middle fingertip to forehead and look ill.

7. <u>WELL</u>: (Opposite of sick, not the deep ones.) Both hands in <u>open-hand, fingers-closed</u> position. Place hands against chest, then bring them forward, closing hands to fists--sort of like a little boy does when he wants you to feel his muscles. Only use both hands simultaneously.

8. <u>WEAK</u>: Left hand in <u>open-hand, fingers-closed</u> position, palm to ceiling and fingertips forward. Right hand in <u>right-angle</u> hand-position, palm to floor. Place fingertips of right hand against center of left palm, then bend and straighten fingers a couple of times.

9. <u>WEAK IN THE HEAD (FEEBLEMINDED)</u>: Place fingertips of right <u>right-angle</u> hand against forehead and bend and straighten them like in WEAK.

10. <u>STRONG</u>: Natural sign. Both hands in "feel my muscles" position.

141

11. <u>POWERFUL</u>: Left hand and arm in "feel my muscles" position, fist clenched, with right hand in <u>open-hand, fingers-closed</u> position, draw a big muscle over muscle of left arm.

12. <u>ANYWAY OR "IT DOESN'T MATTER"</u>: Left hand in <u>right-angle</u> hand-position, palm and fingertips to ceiling. Right hand in <u>open-hand, fingers-closed</u> position. Brush little finger edge of right hand back and forth across fingertips of left hand, letting the fingertips of left hand flap back and forth as you do this.

13. <u>WISH, HUNGER</u>: Right hand in <u>C-hand</u> position, palm to self, thumb on top. Place fingertips and thumb against upper chest and draw hand downward several inches.

14. <u>DESIRE, YEARN</u>: Sign WISH, using both hands (<u>C-hands</u>) one after the other.

15. <u>THIRSTY</u>: Right hand in <u>index-hand</u> position, palm to self and fingertip to ceiling. Place fingertip of right hand against upper part of throat and draw it downward a few inches.

16. <u>VEGETABLES</u>: Spell VEG.

17. <u>POTATOES</u>: Left hand in <u>A-hand</u> position, palm to floor. Right hand in a crooked <u>V-hand</u> position. Place fingertips of right crooked V on back of left palm. (Denotes sticking a fork into a potato.)

18. <u>ONIONS</u>: Right hand in <u>X-hand</u> position. Place knuckle of the X finger against temple and move it (knuckle remaining in place) back and forth from palm down to palm forward position a few times. (Denotes the knuckle rubbing the eye often associated with peeling onions.)

19. <u>TOMATOES</u>: Sign RED, then hold left hand in <u>S-hand</u> position, palm to floor. Bring right hand down and "slice" right index finger against thumb-index side of left fist. (Denotes slicing a tomato.)

20. <u>PUMPKIN</u>: Left hand in <u>S-hand</u> position, palm to floor. Right hand in <u>8-hand</u> position. Flick middle-finger against back of left hand a couple of times (the way someone thumps a melon to see if it is ripe).

21. <u>WATER</u>: Right hand in <u>W-hand</u> position, palm to left and fingertips to ceiling. Place index finger against chin.

22. <u>WATERMELON</u>: Sign WATER, then PUMPKIN.

HOMEWORK ASSIGNMENT

"CLOZE" SENTENCES

Words for which signs will be taught in Lesson 14

1. Apple
2. Peach
3. Cake
4. Cookies, biscuits
5. Bread
6. Butter
7. Milk
8. Tea
9. Buttermilk
10. Vinegar
11. Wine
12. Whiskey
13. Drunk
14. Cook
15. Kitchen
16. Living room
17. Dining room
18. Bedroom

19. Bath
20. Bathroom
21. Fire
22. Table
23. Chair
24. Plate, place
25. Fork
26. Cup
27. Glass
28. Napkin
29. Sweet
30. Sour
31. Bitter, disappoint
32. Sugar
33. Pie
34. Meat
35. Spoon
36. Knife

1. Circle words for which you have been assigned to write sentences.

2. Write sentences on separate sheet and turn in to your instructor at the beginning of the next class session.

NOTES

Signs taught in Lesson 13:

1. Start	9. Feebleminded	16. Vegetables
2. Keys	10. Strong	17. Potatoes
3. Stop	11. Powerful	18. Onions
4. Take	12. Anyway, doesn't	19. Tomatoes
5. Wash	matter	20. Pumpkin
6. Sick	13. Wish, hunger, hungry	21. Water
7. Well	14. Desire, yearn	22. Watermelon
8. Weak	15. Thirsty	

Additional signs learned in class, or additional usages of above signs:

Other notes (including additional homework assigned by instructor if any) and homework recital sentences:

LESSON 14

WORD-DESCRIPTIONS OF SIGNS

1. <u>APPLE</u>: Right hand in <u>X-hand</u> position, palm to floor. Place knuckle of the X against the CHEEK, then twist wrist so that hand rotates back and forth from palm to the floor to palm to the self. Repeat once.

2. <u>PEACH</u>: Right hand in <u>open-and</u> position, palm to self. Place fingertips against cheek (thumb, too), then draw it down and out, closing hand to <u>and-hand</u> position. Almost like EXPERIENCE. (Denotes fuzz on the peach.)

3. <u>CAKE, COOKIES, BISCUITS</u>: Left hand in <u>open-hand, fingers-closed</u> position, palm to ceiling, fingertips to right front. Right hand in <u>C-hand</u> position, with fingers spread. Place fingertips of right hand against left palm, raise them, turn hand slightly, then place them against left palm again.

4. <u>BREAD</u>: Left hand in <u>cupped-hand</u> position, palm to self and fingertips to right. Place left hand close to chest. Right hand in <u>right-angle</u> position, palm to self. Draw fingertips or little finger edge of right fingers down the back of the left hand. (Denotes the slicing of bread in the way European women do it, holding the bread against the chest and drawing a knife downward to slice it.)

5. <u>BUTTER</u>: Left hand in <u>open-hand, fingers-closed</u> position, palm to ceiling and fingertips to right front. Right hand in <u>H-hand</u> position, palm to floor and fingertips to left front. Place fingertips of H against palm of left hand and draw backward as if spreading butter with a knife.

6. <u>MILK</u>: Natural sign. Pantomime milking a cow.

7. <u>TEA</u>: Left hand in <u>A-hand</u> position, right hand in <u>F-hand</u> position. Left palm faces self, right palm faces floor. Place fingertips of F inside circle made by left thumb and index finger and, keeping them there, wiggle hand back and forth. (Denotes the tea bag being dipped in a cup.)

8. <u>BUTTERMILK</u>: Sign BUTTER, then MILK.

9. <u>VINEGAR</u>: Right hand in <u>V-hand</u> position, palm to left and fingertips to ceiling. Place side of index finger against chin. Repeat once.

10. <u>WINE</u>: Right hand in <u>W-hand</u> position, palm to side of cheek. Without touching cheek, but keeping hand close to cheek, fingertips to ceiling, describe small circles.

11. WHISKEY: Both hands in index-hand position BUT with little fingers extended too. Palms facing each other, fingertips to right and left fronts. Place little finger of right hand on top of index finger of left hand. Repeat once. (Denotes measuring fingers of whiskey.)

12. DRUNK: Right hand in 4-hand position, palm to floor and fingertips to left. Moving from right to left, wiggle fingers across the forehead, without actually touching forehead.

13. COOK: Both hands in open-hand, fingers-closed position, fingertips to right and left fronts. Left hand palm to ceiling, right hand palm to floor. Place right hand on left hand, then turn right hand and place back of right hand against left palm.

14. KITCHEN: Sign COOK, then with both hands in open-hand, fingers-closed position, fingertips forward, palms facing each other but about eight to ten inches apart, move hands so that left hand is near body, palm to body, and right hand is eight to ten inches in front of left hand, palm to body. This sign, the last part of it after COOK, means ROOM.

15. ROOM: Both hands in open-hand, fingers-closed (or R-hand) position, palms facing each other (separated by about eight to ten inches). Bring left hand (unchanged as to hand-position) close to waist, palm to self, while simultaneously moving right hand (changes ro right-angle hand) forward to a position about eight to ten inches directly in front of left hand, with right palm facing left. (Forms a square with the hands.)

16. DINING ROOM: Sign EAT, then ROOM.

17. LIVING ROOM: Sign LIVE, then ROOM.

18. BEDROOM: Place right hand, in open-hand, fingers-closed position, fingers to ceiling, against cheek, then sign ROOM.

19. BATH: A-hands either side of upper chest. Rub up and down.

20. BATHROOM: Sign BATH, then ROOM.

21. FIRE: Both hands in open-and-hand position, palms and fingertips to ceiling. Moving hands alternately, waggle fingers, and raise and lower each hand a few inches while waggling. (Denotes flames rising and falling.)

22. TABLE: Both hands in open-hand, fingers-closed position. Both palms to floor. Right hand fingertips face left and left hand fingertips face right. Place right hand palm on top of back of left hand and pat it a couple of times.

23. CHAIR: Same as SIT.

24. PLATE, PLACE: Both hands in P-hand position, palms to floor, fingertips forward. Touch middle fingers of P's together, describe horizontal circle, bringing hands back toward body, then touch fingertips together again. Same fingertips, I mean.

25. FORK: Left hand in <u>open-hand, fingers-closed</u> position, palm to ceiling, right hand in <u>V-hand</u> position. Touch V fingertips to palm, lift them, turn hand, then touch palm again. (This sign is made like MEAN, except that V fingers are used instead of M fingers.)

26. CUP: Left hand in <u>open-hand, fingers-closed</u> position, palm to ceiling and fingertips to right front. Right hand in <u>C-hand</u> position, palm to left. Place little finger edge of right hand in center of left palm.

27. GLASS: Sign CUP, then raise right hand an inch or two above left palm.

28. NAPKIN: Right hand in <u>B-hand</u> position, palm to self and fingertips to ceiling. Move hand back and forth from right to left and back in front of lips in a wiping gesture. Do not touch lips, but keep fingers close to lips. (Can also be made with hand in <u>A-hand</u> position.)

29. SWEET: Right hand in <u>B-hand</u> position, palm to self and fingertips to ceiling. Place fingertips on upper part of chin, then draw them downward, ending with right hand in <u>right-angle hand</u> position. Repeat once.

30. SOUR: Right hand in <u>index-hand</u> position, palm to left. Placing fingertips of index finger against chin, rotate hand until palm is to self. (Denotes the screwing up of the mouth against sourness.)

31. BITTER: (Also means DISAPPOINT and MISS, as in "I missed you when you were away.") Right hand in <u>index-hand</u> position, palm to self. Bounce index finger off chin once.

32. SUGAR: Signed like SWEET, but instead of using <u>B-hand</u> position for the hand, you use the <u>U-hand</u> position.

33. PIE: Both hands in <u>open-hand, fingers-closed</u> position, left palm to ceiling, and right hand with palm to left. With little finger edge of right hand, cut a "wedge" from left palm.

34. MEAT: Left hand in <u>open-hand, fingers-closed</u> position, but with <u>thumb extended</u> (exposing membrane between thumb and palm), and palm to self; right hand in <u>F-hand</u> position (but with index finger and thumb separated by about an inch), palm to floor. With thumb and index finger of right hand, take a good grip on the membrane between thumb and palm of left hand, and shake both hands slightly <u>as a unit</u>. (<u>Note</u>: Do not waggle them separately. The hands move simultaneously, and remain together.)

35. SPOON: Left hand in <u>open-hand, fingers-closed</u> position, palm to ceiling and fingertips toward right; right hand in <u>H-hand</u> position, palm to ceiling and fingertips pointing to left center. With the fingertips of right hand, "scoop" imaginary food out of center of left palm (as if you were spooning up ice cream).

36. KNIFE: Both hands in <u>index-hand</u> position, palms facing half-way between self and each other, and fingertips pointing toward floor (almost). With right index finger, "whittle" the left index finger as if you were sharpening a pencil with a knife. (Almost like the widely used "shame on you" gesture--except that fingertips point to floor, and palms of hands <u>face each other</u> almost. The inner edge of the right index finger scrapes the <u>thumb-side edge</u> of the left index finger.)

Words for which signs will be taught in Lessons 15 and 16

1. Curlers (hair)
2. Forehead
3. Cheeks
4. Gleam
5. Lotion
6. Potion (medicine)
7. Ocean
8. Cleansing
9. Pore
10. Closing
11. Cream (face)
12. Powder
13. Rouge
14. Lips
15. Eyed (gazed)
16. Untied
17. Bit (a little)
18. Wide
19. Girdle
20. Hips
21. Clothes

22. Dresses
23. Old fashioned
24. Slippers
25. Kippers (fish)
26. Frocks
27. Zippers
28. Just (recently)
29. Up (get up)
30. Sniveling
31. Cold (in the head)
32. Hope
33. Nerves
34. Steady
35. Rock
36. View
37. True (sure)
38. True (honest)
39. Hell
40. Damn
41. Shock
42. Continue, stay

No "Cloze" sentences required for these except for your own practice—unless instructor requires it.

NOTES

Signs taught in Lesson 14:

1.	Apple	13.	Drunk	25.	Fork
2.	Peach	14.	Cook	26.	Cup
3.	Cake	15.	Kitchen	27.	Glass
4.	Cookies, biscuits	16.	Living room	28.	Napkin
5.	Bread	17.	Dining room	29.	Sweet
6.	Butter	18.	Bedroom	30.	Sour
7.	Milk	19.	Bath	31.	Bitter, disappoint
8.	Tea	20.	Bathroom	32.	Sugar
9.	Buttermilk	21.	Fire	33.	Pie
10.	Vinegar	22.	Table	34.	Meat
11.	Wine	23.	Chair	35.	Spoon
12.	Whiskey	24.	Plate, place	36.	Knife

Additional signs learned in class, or additional usages of above signs:

Other notes (including additional homework assigned by instructor if any) and homework recital sentences.

LESSONS 15 AND 16

"EYE-OPENER"

By Richard Armour

Young Man, have you seen her in curlers
With forehead and cheeks all a-gleam
With lotions, and potions, and who knows what oceans
Of cleansing and pore-closing creams?

Young Man, have you seen her unpowdered
Unrouged on the cheeks and the lips
Have you eyed her untied
And a good bit more wide
Ungirdled, I mean, at the hips?

Young Man, have you seen her in work clothes
In dresses outmoded and old
In slippers like kippers
And frocks without zippers
Just up from a sniveling cold?

You haven't? Then young man, here's hoping
Your nerves are as steady as rock
When you do get a view
Of your true love that's true
You're in for a hell of a shock!

WORD-DESCRIPTIONS OF SIGNS

1. CURLERS: Both hands in the R-hand position, palms to head and fingertips
   facing each other. Beginning at the hairline (forehead), rotate both
   hands from palms to head to palms forward position, moving hands toward the nape of the neck (over the top of the head) to denote the rol-
   lers women wind hair on nowadays.

2. FOREHEAD: Right hand in open-hand, fingers-closed position, palm to forehead. Pass the fingertips of the hand across the forehead. (Fingertips point to left.)

3. CHEEKS: Pinch cheek with right hand (thumb and crooked index finger of
   hand do the pinching).

4. A'GLEAM (SHINY): Left hand in open-hand, fingers-closed position, palm
   to floor and fingertips to right front. Right hand in 5-hand position,
   with middle finger bent slightly toward palm. Touch fingertip of middle finger of right hand to back of left palm, then raise right hand,
   waggling the fingers of right hand as you raise it several inches.

5. LOTIONS: Left hand in cupped-hand position, palm to ceiling and fingertips to right front. With right hand in C-hand position, palm to left,
   pantomime pouring lotion out of a bottle into palm of left hand, then
   make a washing motion as if smoothing lotion on the hands.

6. MEDICINE, POTIONS: Left hand in open-hand, fingers-closed position, palm
   to ceiling, with fingertips to right front. Right hand in 5-hand position with middle finger bent slightly toward palm (as in SHINY). Touch
   fingertip of middle finger of right hand to center of left palm and move
   it in tiny circles, keeping it against left palm.

7. OCEAN: Sign WATER (right hand in W-hand position, palm to left and fingertips to ceiling, touch index finger of "W" to lips), then with both
   hands in open-hand, fingers-closed position, palms to floor and fingertips forward, move both hands up and down, moving them also sideways to
   denote big ocean waves.

8. CLEANSING: Sign CLEAN twice, quickly.

9. PORE: Spell out.

10. CLOSING: Sign CLOSE with both hands in B-hand position, palms toward each
    other and fingertips to ceiling, turn hands to palm forward position,
    index sides of hands touching. (Denotes closing of double doors.)

11. CREAM (face cream, not dairy cream): Left hand in cupped-hand position,
    palm to ceiling and fingertips to right front. With right hand in
    cupped-hand position, "scoop" a wad of "cream" out of cupped left palm,
    then open right hand to open-hand, fingers-closed position, palm to
    face, and spread "it" on your cheek.

12. (UN)POWDERED: (Sign NOT) then with right hand in B-hand position, palm to face and fingertips to ceiling, go through the motions of powdering the nose from cheek to cheek across the bridge of the nose.

13. (UN)ROUGED: (Sign NOT) then with right hand in and-hand position, touch fingertips to cheek and make circles as if you were applying a rouge puff to your cheek.

14. LIPS: Run forefinger (index finger) along the lips (if you are a girl, keep your finger a fraction of an inch away or you'll smear your lipstick).

15. EYED: With right hand in index-hand position, palm to face and finger-tip to ceiling, touch index finger to cheek under eye, then open right hand to V-hand position, and turn it around so it is palm to floor, fingertips forward. Raise and lower fingertips (denotes the eyes look-ing someone up and down).

16. (UN)TIED: (Sign NOT) then with both hands in F-hand position, palms facing each other and fingertips of extended fingers facing forward, pantomime tying a ribbon in a bow.

17. BIT: With right hand in a modified X-hand position, pick little bits out of your index fingertip with your thumbnail (almost like a coin-flipping gesture, but not as emphatic as in the sign for FAST. (Also means LITTLE.)

18. WIDE: Sign BIG, but keep palms flat and make the gesture strictly horizontal.

19. (UN)GIRDLED: (Sign NOT) then with both hands in A-hand position, thumbs on top and palms facing stomach, pretend you are trying to make a tight girdle meet in the middle of your stomach.

20. HIPS: With both hands in open-hand, fingers-closed position, pat your-self on the sides of your hips.

21. CLOTHES: Both hands in 5-hand position, palms to body and fingertips facing each other. Place your thumbs on each side of your chest, then draw them down your chest, turning hands as you do this so that you end the sign with fingertips pointing to floor. Repeat this once, quickly. (Also means DRESS, FROCK, and so forth.)

22. DRESSES: Same as CLOTHES.

23. OLD-FASHIONED (outmoded): Sign OLD, then A LONG TIME AGO (using both hands for A LONG TIME AGO).

24. SLIPPERS: Left hand in B-hand position, palm to floor and fingertips to right front. Right hand in C-hand position, palm to floor and fingertips to floor. Place palm of right hand against fingertips of left hand (enclosing left hand in the "C"), then draw it back toward wrist.

25. KIPPERS (sign for FISH): Both hands in open-hand, fingers-closed position, left palm facing self and right palm facing left. Place fingertips of left hand against right wrist (right fingertips facing forward), then wave fingertips of right hand back and forth from left to right and back. (Denotes the way a fish swims in water.)

26. FROCKS: Sign CLOTHES.

27. ZIPPERS: Pantomime a woman trying to close a zipper, holding the bottom of the zipper with your left hand, while the right hand, gripping a zipper tab, closes the zipper at the side of the dress (left side, by the way).

28. JUST (as in "just a few minutes ago"): Right hand in X-hand position, palm facing back over right shoulder, fingertip ditto. Place finger-side of index finger against cheek and straighten then crook the index finger.

29. UP (as in arise from bed): Left hand in open-hand, fingers-closed position, palm to ceiling, fingertips to right front. Right hand in crooked V-hand position, palm to ceiling and knuckles forward. Bring sign with right hand alongside but not touching left hand, then turn right hand to palm downward position and place fingertips of "V" in center of left palm. (Almost like AGAIN.)

30. SNIVELING: Both hands in B-hand position, with fingers spread. Palms facing body and fingertips facing each other. Alternately brush index fingers downward (right, then left, then right, then left) against the side of the nose.

31. COLD: Right hand in A-hand position with thumb extended, palm to body. Pinch nose between thumb and index finger as if wiping the nose. Repeat once.

32. HOPE: (HOPING is signed the same way.) Sign THINK, then WAIT. WAIT is signed like this: Both hands in right-angle hand-position, with fingers slightly spread. Left hand is several inches out from the body. Right hand is close to the body. Fingertips and palms face each other. Wave fingertips of both hands up and down simultaneously. (Also means EXPECT.)

33. NERVES: Both hands in 5-hand position, palms to body and fingertips to floor. Hold both hands near the upper chest, then move them downward, waggling fingers alternately as you move them downward.

34. STEADY, QUIET: Place index finger of right hand in a "shhh" gesture against lips, then both hands in open-hand, fingers-closed position, palms to floor and fingertips forward. Move both hands smoothly away from each other, horizontally.

35. ROCK: Sign HARD, using S-hand position, not the crooked X-hand.

36. VIEW: Sign EYED.

37. TRUE: Right hand in index-hand position, palm to left. Place side of
     index finger against chin, then move it upward until fingertip is
     level with the nose. (Also means SURE.)

38. TRUE: Sign the above TRUE, then follow it with left hand in open-hand,
     fingers-closed position, palm to ceiling and fingertips to right
     front. Right hand in H-hand position (for HONEST), palm to left and
     fingertips forward. Place side of middle finger in left palm near
     the heel of the hand, then move it forward to the fingertips of left
     hand. (This sign is also used for HONEST.)

39. HELL: Right hand in H-hand position, palm to ceiling, and fingertips
     forward. Move whole hand abruptly sideways, from center front to
     the right.

40. DAMN: Similar to HELL above except that D-hand is used, and palm faces
     floor, not ceiling.

41. SHOCK: Both hands in A-hand position, palms to floor and knuckles for-
     ward. Begin sign with hands parallel but not touching, then separate
     them widely, doing so in an abrupt, vigorous motion, stopping the
     movement abruptly when hands are about eighteen inches or two feet
     apart. Look stunned!

42. CONTINUE, STAY: Both hands in A-hand position, thumbs extended, and
     palms to floor. Place ball of right thumb on top of left thumbnail,
     and push both hands downward and forward a few inches (STAY), or
     forward several inches (CONTINUE).

HOMEWORK ASSIGNMENT

"CLOZE" SENTENCES

Words for which signs will be taught in Lesson 17

1.	Busy	14.	Visit
2.	Idle	15.	Enjoy
3.	Lazy	16.	Rather
4.	Doubt	17.	Almost
5.	Cheap	18.	Easy
6.	Expensive	19.	Responsible, responsibility
7.	Dry	20.	Balance
8.	Wet	21.	Obey
9.	False	22.	Disobey
10.	Liar	23.	Dismay
11.	Smart	24.	Disgust
12.	Arrive	25.	Burden
13.	Leave (depart)		

1. Circle words for which you have been assigned to write sentences.

2. Write sentences on separate sheet and turn in to your instructor at the beginning of the next class session.

NOTES

Signs taught in Lesson 15:

1. Curlers (hair)	15. Eyed (gazed)	29. Up (get up)
2. Forehead	16. Untied	30. Sniveling
3. Cheeks	17. Bit (a little)	31. Cold (in the head)
4. Gleam	18. Wide	32. Hope
5. Lotion	19. Girdle	33. Nerves
6. Medicine, potions	20. Hips	34. Steady
7. Ocean	21. Clothes	35. Rock
8. Cleansing	22. Dresses	36. View
9. Pore	23. Old fashioned	37. True (sure)
10. Closing	24. Slippers	38. True (honest)
11. Cream (face)	25. Kippers (fish)	39. Hell
12. Powder	26. Frocks	40. Damn
13. Rouge	27. Zippers	41. Shock
14. Lips	28. Just (recently)	42. Continue, stay

Additional signs learned in class, or additional usages of above signs:

Other notes (including additional homework assigned by instructor if any)
and homework recital sentences:

BREATHER SESSION NOTES

New signs learned:

Other notes:

LESSON 17

WORD-DESCRIPTIONS OF SIGNS

1. <u>BUSY</u>: Sign WORK several times, using brief, short movements and moving hands back and forth from left to right.

2. <u>IDLE</u>: Hook thumbs of <u>5-hands</u> into imaginary suspenders and waggle fingers.

3. <u>LAZY</u>: Right hand in <u>L-hand</u> position, palm to self and index finger to ceiling. Pound your palm a couple of times against your left upper chest.

4. <u>DOUBT</u>: Both hands in <u>A-hand</u> position, palms to floor. Move each hand up and down alternately.

5. <u>CHEAP</u>: Both hands in <u>open-hand, fingers-closed</u> position. Left palm faces right, fingertips forward. Right hand palm faces floor, finger-tips to left palm. With left hand remaining stationary, brush right fingertips downward across left palm.

6. <u>EXPENSIVE</u>: Sign MONEY, then raise right hand and flick it into <u>open-hand, fingers-closed</u> position as if you had hit its thumb with a hammer.

7. <u>DRY</u>: Like SUMMER and UGLY, but the <u>X-hand</u> finger is drawn in front of the chin.

8. <u>WET</u>: Sign WATER, then with both hands in <u>and-hand</u> position, palms to ceiling, open and close hands from <u>and-hand</u> position to <u>open-and</u> posi-tion and back to <u>and-hand</u> position. Sort of like squeezing a soppy cotton ball between the fingertips.

9. <u>FALSE</u>: Right hand in <u>right-angle index</u> position, palm to left and index fingertip pointing to left. Move index finger across chin from right to left. (Also means LIE.) You can also use <u>right-angle</u> hand-position instead of <u>right-angle index</u> hand-position.

10. <u>LIAR</u>: Sign FALSE, then PERSON.

11. <u>SMART</u>: (a) Right hand in <u>index-hand</u> position, palm forward and index finger pointing to ceiling. Touch index finger to temple then oscil-late it upward.

    (b) With right hand in <u>5-hand</u> position, middle finger bent toward palm, touch tip of middle finger to forehead at temple, then turn it from palm to self to palm forward in a brisk motion.

(c) (Slang version) With right hand in <u>C-hand</u> position, palm to left, place the length of the thumb against the forehead--thus measuring a "thickness" of "brains" bigger than ordinary. This is sometimes elaborated upon by piling "C" upon "C," moving the hands in steps away from the head. Your teacher can demonstrate this version.

12. <u>ARRIVE</u>: Both hands in <u>right-angle</u> hand-position, palms toward each other and knuckles forward. With left hand several inches in front of right hand (and remaining stationary), bring right hand forward and place backs of right fingers against palms of left fingers. Also is used for GET in sentences like--"When I <u>get</u> home, I'm going to go right to bed."

13. <u>LEAVE (depart)</u>: Both hands in <u>open-hand, fingers-closed</u> (or <u>cupped-hand</u>) position. Palms to floor. Bring both hands backward toward body, closing them to <u>A-hand</u> position, palms forward and knuckles to ceiling.

14. <u>VISIT</u>: Both hands in <u>V-hand</u> position, palms to self, fingertips to ceiling. Move each hand in circles alternately. Signed somewhat like PEOPLE.

15. <u>ENJOY</u>: Sign PLEASE.

16. <u>RATHER</u>: Sign PLEASE, then -EST, like the ending gesture of BEST.

17. <u>ALMOST</u>: Exactly the opposite of THAN. Both palms face ceiling, and right hand comes from below the left hand, striking left fingertips as it rises.

18. <u>EASY</u>: Sign ALMOST twice, with hands relaxed.

19. <u>RESPONSIBLE, RESPONSIBILITY</u>: Right hand in <u>R-hand</u> position, palm to self and fingertips on shoulder and lower shoulder slightly.

20. <u>BALANCE</u>: Almost exactly like MAYBE, except that palms face floor.

21. <u>OBEY</u>: Right hand in <u>A-hand</u> position, palm to self. Touch thumb to temple, then lower hand, opening it to <u>open-hand, fingers-closed</u> position, palm to ceiling and fingertips forward.

22. <u>DISOBEY</u>: Sign THINK, then right hand in <u>A-hand</u> position, palm to self turn hand to palm outward vigorously.

23. <u>DISMAY</u>: Right hand in <u>clawed-hand</u> position, palm to self and fingertips to chest. Place fingertips against chest and move them in a circle, keeping fingertips against chest.

24. <u>DISGUST</u>: Sign DISMAY.

25. <u>BURDEN</u>: Sign RESPONSIBLE, but use <u>right-angle</u> hand instead of <u>R-hand</u>. Can also be made with both hands (both on one shoulder) for emphasis.

HOMEWORK ASSIGNMENT

"CLOZE" SENTENCES

Words for which signs will be taught in Lesson 18

1. Agree
2. Disagree
3. Angry
4. Accept, receive
5. Reject, decline
6. Honor
7. Respect
8. Humble, simple, plain
9. Proud
10. Pass
11. Race
12. Idea

13. Imagination
14. Memorize
15. Reason
16. Inform
17. Information
18. Wait
19. California
20. New York
21. Chicago
22. Detroit
23. San Francisco
24. St. Louis

1. Circle words for which you have been assigned to write sentences.

2. Write sentences on separate sheet and turn in to your instructor at the beginning of the next class session.

NOTES

Signs taught in Lesson 17:

1.	Busy	10.	Liar	18.	Easy
2.	Idle	11.	Smart	19.	Responsible, responsibility
3.	Lazy	12.	Arrive		
4.	Doubt	13.	Leave (depart)	20.	Balance
5.	Cheap	14.	Visit	21.	Obey
6.	Expensive	15.	Enjoy	22.	Disobey
7.	Dry	16.	Rather	23.	Dismay
8.	Wet	17.	Almost	24.	Disgust
9.	False			25.	Burden

Additional signs learned in class, or additional usages of above signs:

Other notes (including additional homework assigned by instructor if any):

LESSON 18

WORD-DESCRIPTIONS OF SIGNS

1. <u>AGREE</u>: Sign THINK, then ALIKE, <u>keeping hands</u> separated by a few inches instead of touching index fingers together.

2. <u>DISAGREE</u>: Sign THINK, then ENEMY, omitting the -ER part of the ENEMY sign.

3. <u>ANGRY</u>: Right hand in <u>clawed-hand</u> position, palm to self and knuckles facing left. Place fingertips and thumb-tip against chest, then drag the hand upward and off the chest, keeping palm toward body.

4. <u>ACCEPT, RECEIVE</u>: Both hands in <u>open-and</u> position, palms facing each other. Place both thumbs against chest, then close hands to <u>and-hand</u> position.

5. <u>REJECT, DECLINE</u>: Left hand in <u>open-hand, fingers-closed</u> position, palm to ceiling and fingertips to right front. Right hand in <u>cupped-hand</u> or <u>right-angle</u> hand-position, palm to self and fingertips to ceiling. Place right fingertips against chin, then place them against left palm near heel of hand, then brush them across left hand palm and fingers and off the ends of the fingers. (Denotes wiping something off a slate.) (Similar to EXCUSE.)

6. <u>HONOR</u>: Right hand in <u>H-hand</u> position, palm to left and fingertips to ceiling. Place index finger against forehead, then lower hand out and away from face, keeping fingers in <u>H-hand</u> position.

7. <u>RESPECT</u>: Exactly like HONOR, but use <u>R-hand</u> position instead of <u>H-hand</u> position.

8. <u>HUMBLE, SIMPLE, PLAIN</u>: Right hand in <u>index-hand</u> position. Place right finger against lips (in a "Shh" gesture), then sign SOME. (Part-type SOME, not somebody-type.)

9. <u>PROUD</u>: Right hand in <u>A-hand</u> position, palm to floor and knuckles pointing to left. Place thumbnail against chest near waist and draw hand upward. (This is derived from the buttons popping off a shirt when the thumb is drawn up.)

10. <u>PASS</u>: Both hands in <u>A-hand</u> position, palms facing each other and knuckles forward. With left hand in advance of right hand, bring right hand forward and pass left hand.

LESSON 19

BELIEVE ME IF ALL THOSE ADHERING STRANGE CHARMS . . .
(Parody of "Believe Me if All Those Endearing Young Charms . . .")

Believe me if all those adhering strange charms
Which I gaze on with admiring dismay
Are going to come off on the shoulders and arms
Of this suit I had cleaned just today.

Thou will still be adored, as this moment thou art,
My sweetheart, my loved one, my own.
But I will strongly suppress the emotions I feel
And love you but leave you alone.

'Tis not that thy beauty is any the less,
Nor thy cheeks unaccustomedly gay.
They are lovely, indeed, I will gladly confess,
But I think I should leave them that way.

For the bloom of thy youth isn't on very tight,
and the powder rolls off of thy nose.
So my love is platonic, my dear, for tonight--
For these are my very best clothes.

WORD-DESCRIPTIONS OF SIGNS

1. ADHERING, STICKY: Both hands sign this alternately. First, the left
   hand is in a 5-hand position. When the left hand is in the 8-hand
   position, the right hand is in the 5-hand position. Keep opening
   and closing the hands in 5-hand to 8-hand positions, drawing the
   hands backward from directly in front of you until they are near
   your shoulders. (Denotes the tackiness of a sticky substance.)

2. CHARMS: Spell out, usually, but in poems and songs, sign BEAUTIFUL or
   ATTRACT.

3. ADMIRING: First, touch your nose with your right index finger, then:
   left hand in open-hand, fingers-closed position, palm to ceiling and
   fingertips to front. Right hand in 20-hand position, palm to floor,
   fingertips forward. Place thumb of right hand near base of left
   palm, then slide it forward, opening and closing index finger and
   thumb as you slide it. (Slang sign. Denotes the nose hitting the
   floor and bouncing when someone falls hard for someone else.)

4. WONDERFUL: Sign like SUNDAY, but have the hands near the shoulders and
   be more emphatic about the sign.

5. ADMIRING: (Formal) Sign THINK, then WONDERFUL.

6. COME OFF: With right hand in open-and hand-position, palm and fingertips to left, place back of thumb against lower left arm then close
   hand to and-hand position. Then raise the hand and place it a few
   inches closer to the elbow and repeat the closing of the hand. Repeat twice more, ending near the shoulder. (For this poem only.)

7. SUPPRESS: Left hand in S-hand position, palm to right self and thumb
   on top. Right hand in open-hand, fingers-closed position, palm to
   floor and fingertips to left front. Place right palm on top of left
   fist and lower both hands abruptly. (Push left hand down with right
   palm, in other words.)

8. EMOTIONS: Both hands in A-hand position, palms to self. Place fingers
   against chest, then move both hands upward, opening hands to 5-hand
   position, palms still to self and fingertips to ceiling.

9. UNACCUSTOMEDLY: Sign NOT LIKE ALWAYS.

10. GAY: Both hands in 5-hand position, middle fingers slightly bent toward
    palms, palms forward and fingertips to ceiling. Start sign with hands
    in front of face (but several inches in front, please), then oscillate
    hands backward and upward several inches.

11. INDEED: Sign SURE.

12. <u>CONFESS</u>: Sign MY, then brush hand upward slightly and bring it forward
a couple of inches, ending with hand in <u>open-hand, fingers-closed</u>
position, palm to ceiling and fingertips to left front, a few inches
in front of chest. (Be careful with this sign--you can butcher it
up and make it into VOMIT very easily.)

13. <u>BLOOM</u>: Both hands in <u>and-hand</u> position, palms and fingertips to each
other and knuckles to ceiling. Place both thumbs together, fingertips touching them, <u>keeping thumbs together</u>, open hands and spread
fingers to <u>open-and</u> position.

14. <u>MEETING</u>: Opposite of BLOOM. Have hands in <u>open-and</u> position, thumbs
touching, then close hands to <u>and-hand</u> position, fingertips touching.
Repeat once.

15. <u>TIGHT</u>: Both hands in <u>A-hand</u> position, left hand palm to floor, right
hand palm to left front. Cross wrists and place front of right wrist
on back of left wrist and waggle right fist back and forth. (Like a
person trying to get free when his wrists are tied together.)

16. <u>ROLLS OFF OF</u>: Both hands in <u>V-hand</u> position. Alternately touch index
fingers of each hand to the side of the nose then drop hand, ending
sign with hands palm up, fingertips forward. Please note the
<u>alternately</u>.

17. <u>PLATONIC</u>: Sign FRIENDS twice, alternating the fingers on top--first
right hand finger on top, then left hand finger on top.

NOTES

Signs taught in Lesson 19:

1.	Adhering	7.	Suppress	13.	Bloom
2.	Charms	8.	Emotions	14.	Meeting
3.	Admiring (slang)	9.	Unaccustomedly	15.	Tight
4.	Wonderful	10.	Gay	16.	Rolls off of
5.	Admiring (formal)	11.	Indeed	17.	Platonic
6.	Come off	12.	Confess		

Additional signs learned in class, or additional usages of above signs:

Other notes (including additional homework assigned by instructor if any) and homework recital sentences:

APPENDIX

MASTER VOCABULARY LIST

Lesson 1 (page 32):
    (39 signs)

1. And
2. Confused
3. Don't know
4. Goodbye
5. He, him, she, her
   (a), (b), and (c)
6. Hello
7. Himself, herself
8. His, hers
9. How
10. I
11. It (a) and (b)
12. Its
13. Know
14. Me
15. Mine
16. My
17. Myself
18. No
19. Not (a) and (b)
20. Our, ours
21. Ourselves
22. Practice
23. Question mark sign
24. Right (correct)
25. Their
26. They, them
27. Themselves
28. Think
29. Understand
30. We, us
31. What (a) and (b)
32. Wrong
33. Yes
34. You (pl.)
35. You (sing.)
36. Your (pl.)
37. Your (sing.)
38. Yourself
39. Yourselves (a) and (b)

Lesson 2 (page 45):
    (32 signs)

40. About
41. Am, are, is, be
    (a) and (b)
42. But
43. Call (named)
44. Call (phone)
45. Call (summon)
46. Did you, do you, etc.
47. Different
48. Dumb, stupid, ignorant
    (a) and (b)
49. Fingerspelling
50. Friday
51. Introduce
52. Language
53. Long time ago, a
54. Monday
55. Name
56. Now
57. Same, alike (a), (b),
    and (c)
58. Saturday
59. Sign
60. Story, sentence
61. Sunday
62. Tell, say, said
63. Thursday
64. To
65. Today
66. Tuesday
67. Was, were (new signs)
68. Was, past, back, ago,
    before (a) and (b)
69. Wednesday
70. Will, would, future,
    next
71. Word

Master Vocabulary List, cont'd.

Numbers Lesson (page 51):
(11 signs)

72. Few
73. How many, how much
74. How old
75. Less
76. Many
77. More
78. Much, above (a)
79. Number
80. Old
81. Several
82. Than

Lesson 3 (page 56):
(30 signs)

83. Ability
84. Afternoon
85. All day
86. All night
87. Bad
88. Can
89. Can't, cannot
90. Day
91. Day and night
92. Do, act, behave
93. Evening
94. Excuse (me)
95. Fine
96. Good
97. Lousy
98. Midnight
99. Morning
100. Night (a) and (b)
101. No good
102. Noon
103. Please
104. Sorry
105. Thank (you)
106. That (a) and (b)
107. This
108. This (time concept)
109. Time
110. Tomorrow
111. Very
112. Yesterday

Lesson 4 (page 63):
(42 signs)

113. Afterwhile, later
114. Again
115. College
116. --er sign
117. Experience
118. Expert, skill
119. For
120. Get
121. Have (possessive)
122. Help
123. High school
124. Hour
125. Job
126. Last month
127. Last night
128. Last week
129. Last year
130. Learn
131. Minute, second
132. Month
133. Must
134. Necessary, etc.
135. Next month
136. Next week
137. Next year
138. No (none)
139. One month ago
140. School
141. Slow
142. Student
143. Teach
144. Teacher
145. This afternoon
146. This evening
147. This morning
148. Today (b)
149. Two years ago
     (up to 5)
150. Two (up to 5) years
     from now
151. University
152. Week
153. Work
154. Year

Course Number
Instructor

OUTSIDE ASSIGNMENT SCHEDULE

Assignment I: Due date:

Assignment II: Due date:

Assignment III: Due date:

Completion of all the following assignments by the due date is <u>required</u> of all students in _____.
<u>(course number and title)</u>

Assignment I:

Construct a calendar of the social, religious, educational, and sporting events arranged by the people in the local "deaf community" for their own amusement or betterment, which will take place during the semester.

Assignment II:

Attend one or more of the activities listed in the calendar constructed in Assignment I. Single out at least one deaf person (NOT the same one that your fellow students single out, <u>please</u>) at this event, and, <u>without making it obvious</u> that it is a required class assignment, engage this deaf person in conversation long enough to elicit the following information about him/her:

1. Name (and spell it correctly--for your instructor probably has a lot of friends among the members of your local deaf community).

2. Occupation

3. Cause of deafness (do not worry about the question seeming to be a "personal" one; it is not considered personal by <u>deaf</u> people).

4. Age at onset of deafness.

5. Marital status.

6. Number of children, ages, sexes.

7. Hobbies.

Write a report of your experience including:

1. Your reactions before, during, and after the event.

2. What modes of communication you used (sign language, fingerspelling, pantomime, pen and paper, and so on), and the relative amount of each you used--both to make yourself understood, and to understand the deaf person with whom you were talking.

3. The required information about the deaf person with whom you conversed. Include also such information as to how well the deaf person could understand you and you him/her, orally or otherwise. Cite examples of the way in which he constructed his language, if at all deviant.

Assignment III:

Prepare a proposal for a project you, as a student taking a course in manual communication (M/C), can initiate and carry out in order to accomplish the goals listed below. (Limit papers to not less than three nor more than ten pages.) Show how the project can be carried out (with adaptations if necessary) in your home communities as well as in the community in which the university is located. Show how the following goals can be attained through your project:

1. Help you, as a student in manual communication, practice your skills while, at the same time, acquiring some insight into what adult deaf people are like.

2. Provide some social, economic, educational, or welfare service to deaf persons in the community which will provide benefits not now provided, or improve existing services to deaf people in some way.

It would be helpful if, when writing your reports and proposals, you all follow a standardized format in writing. (Typed papers are preferred--on standard-weight paper, not flimsy paper--but neatly handwritten reports will be accepted.)

For Assignment I, a graphtype calendar of events is required.

In writing your report on Assignment II, please present the information required in the same order in which it is given in the description of the assignment on the preceding page. (Note: A cold-blooded, factual description of your reactions is NOT wanted. You will get static from your instructor if you follow such a format as "Reactions before: Scared spitless. Reactions during: Nervous. Reactions after: Relieved." For some newcomers to the field of deafness, this is one of the toughest assignments they can be called upon to perform for the first time, deliberately going up to and engaging in conversation with a deaf stranger, but one of the most rewarding in the long run. Writing about it often helps you to view the experience in the proper perspective and, as the psychologists would say, helps you to cathart any residual "trauma" still lurking about in your psyche.)

For Assignment III, the preferred style of presentation is that outlined in the APA Publications Manual. Briefly, the format should follow the pattern below.

I. Introduction. (Cite what exists in the area in which you are interested in inaugurating a project, on local, state, and/or national levels.)

II. Justification. (Justify your project: why it should be inaugurated; whether there is a need for this particular type of service; or why you feel deaf people would benefit from it or enjoy it, and so on.)

III. Procedures. (Explain in detail how you would go about inaugurating your proposal, how you think it could be funded; where you would recruit project staff members; who would help plan and/or conduct the project; how you would publicize it so that deaf people would hear about it and take advantage of it; any problems you might encounter and how you would deal with them.)

IV. Anticipated results. (Explain what you think the results of your project would be.)

V. Replication. (Explain how you would go about setting up a similar project in your home community, or how you would adapt your project to fit the needs of deaf people in your home community.)

Note: If the class elects to work toward a grade, your performance on Assignment III may spell the difference between an A and a B (or a B and a C) if there is any doubt about your performance up to that time.

BIBLIOGRAPHY OF SELECTED BOOKS AND ARTICLES

Note: Prices listed do not include postage or applicable local taxes.

1. Babbini, Barbara E. An Introductory Course in Manual Communication: Fingerspelling and the Language of Signs. Northridge, Calif.: San Fernando Valley State College, 1965 (out of print).

2. Babbini, Barbara E. Manual Communication. A Course of Study Outline for Instructors. Urbana, Ill.: Institute for Research on Exceptional Children, 1971 (available only to instructors in manual communication classes).

3. Becker, V. A. Underwater Sign Language. U.S. Divers Corp., Cat. No. 1919. (Available from author, Supervisor of Physically Handicapped, Public School System, San Francisco, Calif. Price, if any, unknown.)

4. Benson, Elizabeth. Sign Language. St. Paul, Minn.: St. Paul Technical Vocational Institute, 1969 (price unknown, if any).

5. Boatner, Maxine T. A Dictionary of Idioms for the Deaf. U.S. Department of Health, Education, and Welfare, 1967 (available through the NAD, price unknown).

6. Bornstein, H., Hamilton, Lillian B., and Kannapell, Barbara M. Signs for Instructional Purposes. Washington, D.C.: Gallaudet College Press, 1965 (available without cost while supply lasts).

7. Casterline, Dorothy, Croneberg, C.C., and Stokoe, W. C., Jr. A Dictionary of American Sign Language on Linguistic Principles. Washington, D.C.: Gallaudet College Press, 1965 ($6.95).

8. Cissna, R. Basic Sign Language. Jefferson City, Mo.: Missouri Baptist Convention, 1963 (out of print).

9. Davis, Anne. The Language of Signs. New York: Executive Council of the Episcopal Church, 1966 ($4.95).

10. Delaney, T., and Bailey, C. Sing unto the Lord: A Hymnal for the Deaf. Hymns translated into the language of signs. St. Louis, Mo.: Ephphetha Conference of Lutheran Pastors for the Deaf, 1959 ($2.00).

11. Falberg, R. M. The Language of Silence. Wichita, Kan.: Wichita Social Services for the Deaf, 1963 ($2.75).

12. Fant, L. J. Say It with Hands. Washington, D.C.: Amer. Ann. of the Deaf, Gallaudet College, 1964 ($3.50).

13. Fauth, Bette L. and W. W. A Study of the Proceedings of the Convention of American Instructors of the Deaf, 1850-1949, Chap. XIII: The Manual Alphabet. Amer. Ann. of Deaf, 96, 292-296, March, 1951 (reprints may be available without cost).

186

14. Fauth, Bette L. and W. W. Sign Language. Amer. Ann. of Deaf, 100, 253-263, March, 1955 (reprints may be available without cost).

15. Fellendorf, G. W., ed. Bibliography on Deafness. A selected index. Volta Rev., A. G. Bell Assoc., Washington, D.C., 1966 (no list price).

16. Geylman, I. The Sign Language and Hand Alphabet of Deaf Mutes. In Proceedings of the Workshop on Interpreting for the Deaf. Muncie, Ind.: Ball State Teachers College, 1964, 62-90 (available in limited supply without cost).

*17. Greenberg, Joanne. In this Sign. Fiction. New York: Holt, Rinehart, and Winston, 1971 ($5.95).

**18. Guillory, LaVera M. Expressive and Receptive Fingerspelling for Hear- Adults. Baton Rouge, La.: Claitor's Book Store, 1966 ($1.00).

19. Higgins, D., C.S.S.R. How to Talk to the Deaf. Newark, N.J.: Mt. Carmel Guild, Archdiocese of Newark, 1959 (no price listed).

20. Hoeman, H. W., ed. Improved Techniques of Communication: A Training Manual for Use with Severely Handicapped Deaf Clients. Bowling Green, Ohio: Bowling Green State Univ., 1970 (no price listed).

21. Kosche, M. Hymns for Singing and Signing. 116 Walnut St., Delavan, Wis., 53115 (date and price unknown).

22. Landes, R. M. Approaches: A Digest of Methods in Learning the Language of Signs. Virginia Baptist General Board, P.O. Box 8568, Richmond, Va., 23226, 1968 ($2.95).

23. Long, J. S. The Sign Language: A Manual of Signs. Reprint. Washington, D.C.: Gallaudet College Bookstore, 1963 (no price listed).

**24. Madsen, W. J. Conversational Sign Language: An Intermediate Manual. Washington, D.C.: Gallaudet College Bookstore, 1967 ($2.50).

25. Myers, L. J. The Law and the Deaf. Dept. of Health, Education, and Welfare, Washington, D.C., 20201, 1970 (no price listed).

**26. O'Rourke, T. J., dir. A Basic Course in Manual Communication. NAD Com- municative Skills Program, 905 Bonifant St., Silver Spring, Md., 20910, 1971 ($4.50).

27. Peet, Elizabeth. The Philology of the Sign Language. Reprinted pamphlet. Buff & Blue, Gallaudet College, 1921 (available without cost while supply of reprints lasts).

*Recommended additional reading.

**Recommended for purchase as additional reference book or supplementary text.

*28. Quigley, S. P., ed. Interpreting for Deaf People. Workshop report. U.S. Dept. of Health, Education, and Welfare, Washington, D.C., 20201, 1965 (available without cost while supply lasts).

29. Rand, L. W. An Annotated Bibliography of the Sign Language of the Deaf. Unpublished master's thesis. Seattle, Washington: University of Washington, 1962 (may be available by writing the author, c/o Univ. of Wash.).

30. Riekehof, Lottie L. Talk to the Deaf. Springfield, Mo.: Gospel Publishing House, 1963 ($4.95).

31. Roth, S. D. A Basic Book of Signs Used by the Deaf. Fulton, Mo.: Missouri School for the Deaf, 1948 (out of print).

32. Sanders, J. I., ed. The ABC's of Sign Language. Tulsa, Okla.: Manca Press, 1968 ($8.75).

33. Siger, L. C. Gestures, the Language of Signs, and Human Communication. Amer. Ann. of Deaf, 113, 11-28, Jan. 1968 (no price listed).

34. Smith, J. M. Workshop on Interpreting for the Deaf. Workshop report. Muncie, Ind., Dept. of Health, Education, and Welfare, Washington, D.C., 1964 (available without cost while supply lasts).

35. Springer, C. S., C.S.S.R. Talking with the Deaf. Baton Rouge, La.: Redemporist Fathers, 1961 ($2.50).

*36. Stokoe, W. C. Sign Language Structure: An Outline of the Visual Communication Systems of the American Deaf. Research paper. Buffalo, N.Y.: University of Buffalo, 1960 ($2.00).

37. Taylor, Lucille N., ed. Proceedings of the Registry of Interpreters for the Deaf. Conference report. Wisconsin School for the Deaf. Delavan, Wis., 53115, 1965 (available without cost while supply lasts).

*38. Watson, D. O. Talk with Your Hands. Menasha, Wis.: George Banta Pub. Co., 1963 ($5.00).

39. Wisher, P. R. Use of the Sign Language in Underwater Communication. Lithograph. Washington, D.C.: Gallaudet College Bookstore (date and price unknown).

FILMS

1. Episcopal Church Training Films. Audio-Visual Library, The Episcopal Church Center, 815 Second Avenue, New York, N.Y. A series of forty training films on signs in 3mm. cartridge-type reels of approximately

*Recommended additional reading.

*Recommended for purchase as additional reference book or supplementary text.

four minutes playing time each. Religious in orientation. Handbook available (see No. 8, Davis, in list of books and articles). Black and white.

2. <u>Fingerspelling Films</u>. (International Communications Foundation series.) Captioned Films and Media Services for the Deaf, U.S. Office of Education, Washington, D.C., 20201. A series of nine training films on fingerspelling in 3mm. cartridge-type reels of approximately four minutes playing time each. Oriented toward dormitory and rehabilitation counselors. Color.

3. <u>The American Manual Alphabet</u>. (Graphic Films Corp. series.) Captioned Films and Media Services for the Deaf, U.S. Office of Education, Washington, D.C., 20201. A series of thirty training films in fingerspelling in 8mm. cartridge-type reels of approximately four minutes playing time each. Programmed drills in specific letter groups, words, and sentences. Includes tests, examples of faulty techniques, and so on. Color.

4. <u>Pre-Cana Counseling Film</u>. Captioned Films and Media Services for the Deaf, U.S. Office of Education, Washington, D.C., 20201. A single 16mm. signed film dealing with premarital counseling. Religious (Catholic in orientation). Black and white.

5. <u>Say It with Hands</u>. KERA-TV 13, 3000 Harry Hines Blvd., Dallas, Tex., 75201. 16mm. kinescopes of twenty-six half-hour programs providing instruction in manual communication based on Fant's book. (Rental: $10 per half-hour tape. Also available through Captioned Films on loan basis for holders of CFD account numbers. Requires special TV equipment.)

ADDRESSES OF MAJOR DISTRIBUTORS OF BOOKS AND FILMS

National Association of the Deaf
Communicative Skills Program
814 Thayer Avenue
Silver Springs, Maryland 29010

Gallaudet College (Bookstore and Press)
7th and Florida Avenues, N.E.
Washington, D.C. 20002

Department of Health, Education, and Welfare
Rehabilitation Services Administration
Communication Disorders Branch
Washington, D.C. 20201

Captioned Films Distribution Services
Conference of Executives of American Schools for the Deaf
5034 Wisconsin Avenue, N.W.
Washington, D.C. 20016

INDEX OF MASTER VOCABULARY LIST

194